access to politics

BRITISH POLITICS
and
EUROPE

Alan Davies

Series Editor: David Simpson

Hodder & Stoughton

A MEMBER OF THE HODDER HEADLINE GROUP

ACKNOWLEDGEMENTS

The photos on pp 10, 45, 71 and 122 are reproduced with permission of PA News.

Order queries: please contact Bookpoint Ltd, 130 Milton Park, Abingdon, Oxon OX14 4SB. Telephone: (44) 01235 400414, Fax: (44) 01235 400454. Lines are open from 9.00–6.00, Monday to Saturday, with a 24 hour message answering service
Email address: orders@bookpoint.co.uk

British Library Cataloguing in Publication Data
A catalogue record for this title is available from The British Library

ISBN 0 340 720794

First published 1998
Impression number 10   9   8   7   6   5   4   3
Year   2004   2003   2002   2001

Copyright © 1998, Alan Davies

Cover image of the logo of the UK Presidency of the European Union 1998, reproduced by permission of the Foreign and Commonwealth Office

Typeset by Transet Limited, Coventry, England.
Printed in Great Britain for Hodder & Stoughton Educational, a division of Hodder Headline Plc, 338 Euston Road, London NW1 3BH by
The Bath Press, Bath

CONTENTS

PREFACE

A/AS Level syllabuses in Government and Politics aim to develop knowledge and understanding of the political system of the UK. They cover its local, national and European Union dimensions, and include comparative studies of aspects of other political systems, in order to ensure an understanding of the distinctive nature of the British political system. The minimum requirements for comparative study are aspects of systems with a separation of powers, how other systems protect the rights of individuals and how other electoral systems work.

Access to Politics is a series of concise topic books which cover the syllabus requirements, providing students with the necessary resources to complete the course successfully.

General advice on approaching exam questions

To achieve high grades you need to demonstrate consistency. Clearly address all parts of a question, make good use of essay plans or notes, and plan your time to cover all the questions.

Make your answers stand out from the crowd by using contemporary material to illustrate them. You should read a quality newspaper and listen to or watch appropriate programmes on radio and television.

Skills Advice

You should comprehend, synthesise and interpret political information in a variety of forms:

- Analyse and evaluate political institutions, processes and behaviour, political arguments and explanations.
- Identify parallels, connections, similarities and differences between aspects of the political systems studied.
- Select and organise relevant material to construct arguments and explanations leading to reasoned conclusions.
- Communicate the arguments with relevance, clarity and coherence, using vocabulary appropriate to the study of Government and Politics.

David Simpson

1

INTRODUCTION

THE UNITED KINGDOM became a member of the European Union (EU) in 1973. This has been a crucial issue for the UK since the Second World War, because it has had enormous economic, political, diplomatic, cultural and constitutional repercussions. It is difficult to separate these issues: for example, the Single European Act of 1986 promoted a **single economic market** between member countries, which also carried implications for social policy, politics and the constitutions of those states; similarly, the debate over **Economic and Monetary Union** (EMU – which would introduce a single European currency) is sometimes couched in purely economic terms, sometimes in constitutional ones and often in both.

While recognising the interdependence of politics and economics, domestic and foreign policy, it is still necessary to untangle the issues and examine them one at a time.

Key Points

This chapter explores the following issues:

- The key concepts of **federalism, intergovernmentalism, supranationalism,** and **functionalism**.
- The significance of the Treaty of European Union, better known as the Maastricht Treaty.
- The institutions of the European Union.
- Why Europe is important to the UK, and yet why the British often appear at best apathetic about matters European.

THE UK'S PLACE IN EUROPE

The French federalist Jean Monnet, who did more than anyone else to create what is now the European Union, claimed in his memoirs that:

> *'the civilisation of the West needs Britain, and Europe to continue her unique contribution to that civilisation, needs the qualities that reside in the British people'.*

Yet according to the veteran leftwing journalist Ian Aitken writing in the 1990s, 'the tragedy of British politics since the war is that the most crucial issue of the period [Europe] has also been popularly regarded as the most boring'.

It is not just that the UK's place in Europe has not commanded public attention, but that it has become the ultimate political 'turn off'. It was not until 1973, 16 years after the formation of the European Community, that the UK finally joined it; even then, involvement was often less than wholehearted with the result that the UK has been described generally as a 'semi-detached' member and as 'an awkward partner'. The debate in the UK has more often than not been negative, with 'Europe' often portrayed as an alien force, intent on robbing the British people of their very nationhood. It sometimes seems as though, now that the Cold War against Soviet communism is over, a new enemy has been discovered which poses just as grave a threat to British independence – the European Union.

The reality is more mundane. There is no Brussels plot to force the British to abandon their traditions, yet it is impossible to overstate the day-to-day impact on British life of European regulations and directives. From environmental initiatives to action on equality for women; from harmonisation of health and safety standards in industry to the potential imposition of a standard rate of VAT; 'Europe' is affecting the UK in many ways, most of which never receive publicity because they do not correspond to the tabloid stereotypes. For example, the most important legislation concerning equality for women was passed by the British Parliament in the 1970s (the Equal Pay Act 1970 and the Sex Discrimination Act 1975), but pressure from Europe in the 1980s and 1990s has done a great deal to give women protection, whether it be maternity pay for part-time workers or equal retirement ages for men and women.

In a similar way, while the Conservative and Labour governments since the 1970s have effectively taken power away from local government, in many ways the European Union is giving power back to them. Local authorities are often the bodies responsible for implementing European initiatives, such as on the environment. For example, in 1993 Lancashire Council attempted to persuade the European Commission to take the British government to court over its failure to adhere to European standards for beaches. Local authorities are often the recipients of funding, and would benefit most from closer links with Europe.

THE KEY CONCEPTS

- **Europhile** – literally a lover of all things European, and therefore a passionate supporter of further integration leading logically to a federal Europe.
- **Eurosceptic** – a term that became very fashionable in the 1990s. It implies a degree of suspicion over plans for further EU integration, as in opposition to EMU. Some Eurosceptics are willing to reverse integrationist measures already taken. However, this term is not the same as a **Europhobe**, which involves a much greater degree of opposition and a desire to quit the EU.
- **Subsidiarity** – the devolution of power downwards. Decisions are taken, as far as is compatible with efficiency, by the lowest tier of government. When Continental politicians use the term, they imply the maximum decentralisation of power; when Eurosceptics use it, they imply the retention of power by the nation state.
- **Federalism** – a form of government in which power is divided between one central and several regional governments. The classic federal state is the USA where power is divided between the federal government based in the nation's capital, Washington DC, and the 50 state governments, each of which has its own legislature, executive, judiciary and constitution. The Federal Constitution seeks to protect the powers of the states, but even so, during the twentieth century they have tended to lose power to the Federal Government.

  When politicians such as the former President of the European Commission, Jacques Delors, talk of federalism, what they have in mind is a decentralisation of power; when Eurosceptics use the term, they liken it to an all-powerful superstate based in Brussels.
- **Intergovernmentalism** – governments coming together to cooperate over a range of issues without surrendering national sovereignty. In the EU, the Council of Ministers (see p. 8) embodies this principle, which is why Eurosceptics seek to strengthen the Council.
- **Supranationalism** – the concept of political authority rising above the nation state so that sovereignty would be ceded. The European Court of Justice and the European Commission embody this concept, because members are supposed to forget their national loyalties and look at issues from a European perspective.
- **Functionalism** – gradual, incremental cooperation in certain areas (as in the coal and steel community) leading through 'spillover' to cooperation in other areas. It implies a gradualist, practical approach to integration, one traditionally associated with the British.

There is a fairly clear distinction between the British approach to European integration and that of most other member countries. While many of Europe's politicians wish to move towards a **federal** Europe (a **supranational** body), almost all British politicians favour an **intergovernmental** organisation. Many of the member states have federal systems, the most obvious example being Germany, or have strong traditions of regional autonomy as in Italy and Spain. The United Kingdom in contrast is a unitary state in which all legal power flows from one source, the Westminster Parliament. The British have no federal tradition, and federalism is often denounced as leading to a centralisation of European power in Brussels, the home of the EU institutions.

SUPPORT FOR FEDERALISM

Those who *support* a federal Europe argue that federalism involves a sharing of power. For example, the federal government of the United States shares power with the 50 state governments. It controls the currency, provides the nation's defence and foreign policy and helps fund some of the welfare system. However, the states have a very high degree of independence from Washington:

- They raise their own taxes and make decisions about the form of welfare provided.
- They have their own legal systems.
- Some have the death penalty whilst others do not.
- They even have their own constitution and their own State Supreme Court.

The powers of the states are protected by the 10th Amendment to the Federal Constitution which is upheld by the Federal Supreme Court.

One major difference between the two entities, the USA and a 'United States of Europe', is that in the USA there is one official language, English, whereas in a 15-member European Union there is a minimum of 15 different languages. The USA is an enormous country, being 3,000 miles from coast to coast and almost as far from the Canadian border to the border with Mexico; there are enormous climatic differences within the nation and the economies of the differing regions vary greatly. These huge regional differences within the USA are reflected in customs, cuisine and traditions. Even so, the differences within Europe are even greater, with a predominantly Protestant Northern Europe, a predominantly Catholic South; a largely industrial North versus a mostly agricultural South, and a generally prosperous Northern and Western Europe alongside an often less prosperous South and East. Even if a 'United States of Europe' was to be established, there would be striking differences within it so that the removal of national or regional identities would not happen; indeed there would be a 'Europe of the Regions'. Viewed in this light, a federal Europe would leave a high degree of independence for national governments.

OPPOSITION TO FEDERALISM

Those who *oppose* federalism also quote the American example. They stress that under a federal Europe the British nation state would simply become like a US state, ultimately subordinate to the capital, rather than the sovereign independent state it once was and still should be. American states may have their own tax base but they do not control their own currency, and throughout the twentieth century, the states steadily lost power to Washington to the point where critics argue that the USA is a unitary system in disguise. It is precisely the differences between the USA and Europe which sceptics argue make a federal solution inappropriate for Europe. Any attempt to bind nations as different as Greece and Germany, the United Kingdom and Poland into one political entity will inevitably end with friction and fragmentation, when the whole purpose of European integration has been to avoid such tensions.

This disagreement over the connotations of federalism and sovereignty was one of the reasons that the UK was slow to join the European Community, and it was at the heart of the difficulties over the Treaty of European Union.

THE TREATY OF EUROPEAN UNION

The Treaty of European Union was signed in 1991 in Maastricht, and is often referred to as the **Maastricht Treaty**. European enthusiasts regarded it as the third great step in the Community's history after the Treaty of Rome of 1957 (see p. 20) and the Single European Act of 1986 (see p. 30); the creation of a single currency seemed an irreversible step towards real **federation**. The Treaty created a Citizenship of the Union, which means that EU citizens have the right to live and work anywhere within the Union, and can stand for and vote in elections when outside their own country; for example, the former Liberal Party leader, David Steel MP stood as a candidate for the European Parliament in Italy. The Treaty gave more power to the European Parliament (one of the **supranational** elements) and incorporated the principle of **subsidiarity**:

'an ever closer union among the peoples of Europe, where decisions are taken as closely as possible to the citizen'.

The Treaty turned the former European Community (EC) into the European Union (EU), and the member states agreed to co-operate in three main ways:

1 Under the first pillar of the Treaty, the 15 member states are members of the European Community through which they make common decisions on trade, agriculture, fisheries, the environment, energy, transport and the economy. The aim is to create Economic and Monetary Union by 1999. This means the creation of a single central bank issuing a common currency, the Euro. The primary advantage would be the elimination of exchange rate fluctuations leading to more international trade.

2 They have also agreed to work together over foreign policy under the second pillar of the Treaty. Member states can unanimously agree areas over which they will pursue 'joint action'.

3 Finally they work together over justice and home affairs, terrorism, drugs and crime under the third pillar. In addition all member states are now committed to implementing the Social Chapter. In Britain, the then Conservative government opposed it, but the incoming Labour government signed up for it within days of taking office in May 1997.

Both the second and third pillars created by the Treaty were **intergovernmental** so that the Commission (see p. 9) has no real power and unanimity is required. For this reason, the Maastricht Treaty was in many ways a failure from the federalists' viewpoint, and a victory for intergovernmentalists such as the then British Prime Minister, John Major.

THE INSTITUTIONS OF THE EUROPEAN UNION

The 15 member states of the European Union have a total population of 370 million people, more than Japan and the USA combined. It is the largest voluntary and peaceful bloc in the world, and the goals of the EU include:

- the defence of freedom
- democracy
- respect for human rights
- fundamental freedoms and the rule of law
- the creation of an economic and monetary union, including a stable, single currency
- solidarity between the Union's peoples
- the promotion of social and economic progress
- the establishment of a common citizenship
- the development of common foreign and security policy
- cooperation in the fields of justice and home affairs.

In order to achieve its goals, the EU has at its disposal four institutions:

1 the European Parliament
2 the Council of Ministers of the European Union
3 the European Commission
4 the European Court of Justice.

Theoretically the Commission proposes, the Parliament discusses and the Council of Ministers implements policy, but increasingly, especially in foreign policy and home affairs, the Council has all the power. The Parliament, the Commission and the Court of Justice are supranational bodies, while the Council of Ministers is intergovernmental. It is no coincidence that the animosity of the British Eurosceptics is directed towards the former elements, while they wish to strengthen the latter.

THE EUROPEAN PARLIAMENT

The Parliament consists of 626 members, elected every five years. This is the one directly elected part of the European Union, but is also the least powerful; elections to it have so far failed to ignite public interest, especially in the UK. It shares control over the budget with the Council of Ministers, and has co-decision-making powers in many areas, which means it can amend or reject draft law. Even so, it is a forum for debate rather than a policy-making body. There is a serious democratic deficit in a Union which prides itself on being a collection of democratic states. This raises issues of representation and legitimacy. Are the people of Europe *really* involved in the integrative project that has been developing for the last half a century, or is it simply an elite-driven, and therefore illegitimate, concoction?

In every treaty change over the past 20 years, the European Parliament has won extra powers, which is why pressure groups now devote more attention to it. Even so, its power remains very limited. In the words of the British academic Perry Anderton,

'it functions less like a legislature than a ceremonial apparatus of government, providing a symbolic facade.'

It meets in two different places, Brussels and Strasbourg, which is in itself wasteful. Even in 1991 at Maastricht when federalist hopes were running high, the French government insisted on the Parliament continuing to meet some of the time in Strasbourg, when to gain credibility and to remedy the democratic deficit it really needs to be in Brussels, the real power centre of Europe where the Commission is based.

The Maastricht Treaty was supposed to remedy the democratic deficit, but failed to do much more than extend the power of the European Parliament a little. The German government wished to increase its powers, but the British Conservative government opposed all such moves and even the French government refused to alter the balance of power between the Parliament and the Commission and Council of Ministers based in Brussels.

As a result of the Single European Act 1986 (see p. 30) and the Maastricht Treaty 1992, voters at the 1994 European elections were for the first time electing Members of the European Parliament (MEPs) who could exert real influence over European legislation. Yet, a MORI exit poll in the UK found that 70 per cent of British voters thought they were voting 'mostly about the way the government is running the country' and only 21 per cent about 'the parties' policies on Europe'. The list system of election (each party puts forward a list of candidates ranked by the party, and the voter simply votes for one of the lists) which will be used in the UK in 1999 abolishes the link, however vague it has always been, between an MEP and his or her constituents. The average member of the House of Commons represents 66,107 electors, whereas MEPs represent on average 483,571 electors. This raises serious doubts about the representative role of MEPs.

MEPs vote in party blocs, not national ones; this is itself evidence of a supranationalist approach. British Tory MEPs are supposed to be part of the transnational grouping known as the European People's Party (EPP), but they often break with the group. The EPP has a Christian Democratic philosophy very different to the Conservative Party of the 1990s. (The Christian Democrats are the German conservative party, who believe in a 'social market' in which both the employers and the government have responsibilities to ensure the welfare of the workforce. This is very different from the free market approach of the British Conservatives.) Indeed, after William Hague became leader of the Conservative Party in 1997, British Conservative MEPs were instructed to work against integration from *within* the European Parliament. Similarly British Labour MEPs are often out of tune with the rest of the European Socialists, who are much more willing to move in a federalist direction.

Membership of the European Parliament is not seen as a way of making a political career in the UK; it is not an alternative vehicle to Westminster, and is seen by critics as a 'resting place' for second rate politicians. In the 1980s the leftwing Labour MEP Les Huckfield took to hectoring the European Parliament on the inequities of capitalism and its role in it, with a megaphone. Very, very few people in Britain could name their MEP or even name the Euro constituency within which they live. The European Parliament receives precious little attention from the British media.

THE COUNCIL OF MINISTERS

This is the most intergovernmental of the three bodies. It represents the interests of the member states, and concerns itself with all three pillars of the EU. There are 23 different gatherings, dealing with government departments from foreign affairs to the environment. The outcomes are then binding on the national parliaments. If decisions cannot be reached they are referred to the six-monthly meetings of heads of governments, known as the European Council. These were institutionalised in 1974, and although they have no formal basis, these meetings are increasingly seizing the initiative and generate enormous media interest. Meetings of the Council of Ministers are mostly held in Brussels, and as there are 15 member states, there are always 15 members of the Council, whether it be Agriculture Ministers, Foreign Secretaries or Finance Ministers.

Anderton describes the Council of Ministers as

'the utterly misleading name for what are in fact a parallel series of intergovernmental meetings between departmental ministers from each member state, covering policy areas, whose decisions are tantamount to the legislative function of the Community'.

At the Edinburgh Summit of December 1992, the UK government demanded more transparency in Union decision-making, but even so the Council meets in secret (ie, its discussions are rarely made public). It is the only legislature in the democratic world that meets behind closed doors, again signs of a democratic deficit.

One of the results of the Luxembourg Compromise of 1966 was that decisions in the Council of Ministers had to be reached unanimously, so that any one state could exercise a veto. The Single European Act of 1986 changed things once more with far reaching consequences, particularly in its extension of Qualified Majority Voting (QMV). Under QMV, each country is allocated so many votes depending on the size of its population; the UK had 10 out of a total of 76 at the time of the Single European Act. Fifty-four votes were required to approve a measure. This meant that Britain alone could no longer veto a measure, and it needed the support of other countries. Enlargement in 1994 raised more questions about QMV (see Chapter 8).

THE EUROPEAN COMMISSION

The European Commission has 20 Commissioners: two each from the five larger states (France, Germany, the UK, Spain and Italy) and one from each of the remaining ten. They are aided by a relatively small full-time staff of around 16,000. Each Commissioner is served by a cabinet of advisers. Although appointed by national governments, the Commissioners take an oath to serve the Community as a whole, and cannot be recalled by member states. The President is chosen from among the Commission and normally serves more than one term. The French Socialist Jacques Delors served from 1989 to 1994. The President is the public face of the Commission, the closest Europe has to a 'leader'. He/she coordinates the work of the Commission and deals directly with the Council of Ministers and heads of government, eg, by attending meetings of the European Council.

This institution is the *bête noire* of the sceptics because it is supranational. At the time of writing, Britain's two Commissioners are Leon Brittan (Conservative) and Neil Kinnock (Labour). Brittan was appointed in the late 1980s, and Kinnock in the early 1990s. As a Vice President, Brittan is the senior of the two. He was a Cabinet Minister in Margaret Thatcher's government until his resignation in 1986. As Commissioner, there were many occasions when he was out of step with the Tory governments under Margaret Thatcher and John Major; since 1997, he has distanced himself from the anti-Economic and Monetary Union stance taken by the Conservative Party under the leader, William Hague.

In 1990 at the height of the Commission's power, the then President, Jacques Delors had predicted that soon 80 per cent of economic and social legislation in Europe would come from Brussels. It was such talk which led people to see the Commission as the body which ran the Union. This was never the case but has become even less so since Delors's departure in 1994. His replacement as President, Jacques Santer, was approved, very narrowly, by the European Parliament. Santer has a much lower profile than Delors, which is one reason he was chosen, and has promised that the Commission should 'do less, but do it better'.

JACQUES DELORS, PRESIDENT OF THE COMMISSION 1985–94

THE EUROPEAN COURT OF JUSTICE

The European Court of Justice has 15 members, who act independently of the member states. It is often confused with the European Court of Human Rights (ECHR), but in fact the latter has nothing to do with the European Union. The ECHR was set up to interpret the 1950 European Declaration of Human Rights. The European Court of Justice has always had the power to overrule national parliaments. It is able to strike down legislation passed by parliaments if it feels that EU law is contravened, as it did in the Factortame case of 1991 (see p. 55).

WHY HAS THE EU DEVELOPED?

There have been various attempts by political scientists to explain the development of the European Community. What were the most important reasons for its creation? Was it:

1 The role played by key individuals such as Monnet who were consciously trying to move Europe in a **federalist** direction?
2 Or, was it simply a **functional** response to the political, social and economic conditions of the time which necessitated a degree of cooperation over certain issues?

The first interpretation presupposes a degree of direction, a project moving along a predetermined route, occasionally encountering difficulties as with the British reluctance to get involved, but nonetheless confident of eventual success. The second interpretation puts more emphasis on the practical, day-to-day benefits gained from working together so that after a period of time, the states of Western Europe had reached such a degree of interdependence that not only was another war between them unthinkable, but that the project would continue to develop regardless of which particular individuals happened to be in power.

As always with European integration, there is no agreement about why it happened. The same political scientists have difficulty actually describing the organisation that emerged from the process: it is clearly not a state and yet has certain characteristics of a state. It is not too much of simplification to say that those who prefer to see the European Union move towards a supranational goal, see its history in federalist terms. Conversely, those, as in the UK, who prefer an intergovernmental Europe, see the logic of its development as a functional, incremental movement, without grand theorising about the eventual destination.

BRITISH ATTITUDES TOWARDS EUROPE

What do the British public think about this European Union? It is always difficult to gauge public opinion precisely; people may respond to the mood of the moment rather than to rational analysis of long term problems. Polls consistently show a majority unsure about further integration, yet it is also clear that the UK should remain within the EU. According to Geoffrey Martin, head of the European Commission's UK office:

> *'the British have not seen Europe as an opportunity. They regard it as somewhere between an obligation and a mistake.'*

European issues are assumed to bore the majority of the electorate, and yet they have major implications for obvious vote-winning subjects such as the economy, interest rates, the control of inflation, industrial relations, social policy and immigration.

Partly it is a generational issue. Polls taken in early 1997 showed significantly stronger support for British membership of the EU and further integration among younger voters. Presumably those born since the Second World War have a different attitude from the generations brought up when the UK was still a major imperial power; those born since 1973 when the UK became a member are more likely to see themselves as European. British people now are likely to have travelled to Europe on holiday or business, to have had some contact with European cuisine and fashion, to be knowledgeable about European sport (particularly now that so many foreign players play for British football teams), to receive European television via satellite, to drive a European car and perhaps to have studied a modern European language at school, or see their children doing so.

Yet increased familiarity with European culture does not of itself make it easier for the UK to integrate into the European Union. After all, it could be argued that British people are even more familiar with American culture. Indeed, from the 1950s, more and more of British culture was Americanised which may help explain why there was so little resistance to loss of British sovereignty to the USA.

By then,

- the USA had nuclear bases on British soil
- it dominated NATO which was vital to the UK's defence
- it provided much of the technology for the British nuclear deterrent
- it was the major force within the world economy and therefore effectively controlled the International Monetary Fund (IMF) and the World Bank.

None of this aroused much antagonism in the UK, and there is still much greater resistance to the 'threat' from Europe.

British people are generally less insular than in former times, but it is surely no coincidence that people still talk about Britain going 'into' Europe when we have been a member of the Community for 25 years and part of Europe geographically for millennia. Whenever the former Prime Minister, Mrs Thatcher, was isolated at European summits, she was defiantly proud that her position seemed to recreate the 'Dunkirk spirit' of Britain 'standing alone'. The debate over whether the pound should join the EMU seemed to hinge on whether the single currency would bear the Queen's head. Perhaps the concern over the pound shows how a nation's currency is wrapped up in the nation's psyche, so that loss of the national currency seems to threaten national identity, but it is rather ironic, given the German and Greek antecedents of the House of Windsor.

The British people are not unique in their ambivalence towards Europe:

- Norway has twice rejected membership of the EU in referendums.
- Iceland actually quit the EU.
- In December 1992, Switzerland rejected membership of the European Economic Area (in 1991, this had brought together the European Community and European Free Trade Association (EFTA) in a huge internal market).
- France endorsed the Maastricht Treaty by the tiniest of margins in a referendum in 1992.

• Denmark nearly derailed the whole Maastricht Treaty process by voting against it in a referendum.

Meanwhile all the polls show that whatever the willingness of the German political elite to embrace EMU, the German public are much less convinced, while the French people appear willing to take to the streets in mass protest against the tough economic measures imposed by the government to meet the economic requirements (convergence criteria) agreed at Maastricht for joining the EMU.

Equally, the UK's record for implementing EU legislation is actually very good, much better than that of some of the more openly federalist states. It could be argued therefore that the British need no lessons in being good Europeans.

Yet in no other major member state is there so much consistent apathy and antipathy towards European integration. In surveys undertaken in 1995 the opinion poll organisation MORI found that only 37 per cent described Britain's membership as 'a good thing'; 30 per cent believed it to be a 'bad thing'; 57 per cent did not think of themselves as 'European'; and seven times as many people named the USA as our most reliable ally, than any single European country in the same context.

'UP YOURS DELORS'

At the time of British entry in 1973, every national publication supported this. The same was true in 1975. This had all changed by the 1980s and 1990s, with the press owned by media tycoon Rupert Murdoch (*The Sun*, *The News of the World*, *The Times*, *The Sunday Times*) becoming hostile to almost all things European. It is impossible to conceive of the best-selling paper in any other member state devoting its front page to an attack on the President of the European Commission as *The Sun* did with its famous 'Up Yours Delors' headline in the early 1990s. The by-line 'from our diplomatic correspondent' may have signalled that it was tongue in cheek, but even so it smacked of xenophobia. The press happily seize upon the latest examples of European regulation, whether it be the need for straight bananas or the abolition of double decker buses. During the BSE crisis of 1996 in which the sale of British beef was banned worldwide, *The Sun* adopted a prime bullock called Sonny 'to move into the front line of the Cattle of Britain ... and give the Germans a hefty kick in the panzers'.

The press, particularly the tabloids, tend to concentrate on the supposed inequities of the Common Agricultural Policy (CAP) and the Common Fisheries Policy rather than their positive elements. There is little discussion of the way in which the CAP actually helped to keep the common market going in the early days, or how it still maintains food standards, or to the fact that without the CAP, some British farmers could be forced out of business. There is little mention of the fact that Britain's beef farmers received huge amounts of financial aid from Europe because of the BSE crisis.

Similarly there is little discussion of the constructive ways in which the EU affects the UK. The European Regional Development Fund set up in 1975 aids the less affluent parts of the Union which unfortunately includes several areas of the UK, such as parts of Merseyside and parts of the North East of England.

The Social Chapter of the Treaty of European Union is often presented by the press as European meddling in the arrangements of British industry, which, if adopted here, would increase wage costs and increase unemployment. When she was Employment Secretary in the Conservative government, Gillian Shepherd resisted European attempts at regulating working hours on the grounds that British workers must be 'free' to work as many hours as they wish. It could be argued that British workers were entitled to the same degree of protection as their European counterparts, and that ultimately the British economy would benefit from higher workplace standards.

The French government dominated the European Community in its early days, just as the Germans have done as the Community has developed; the Italians and the Benelux countries (Belgium, the Netherlands and Luxembourg) are the most consistently pro-Europe, while the Spanish having shaken off their authoritarian regime in the mid-1970s were anxious to show their mainstream European credentials by joining at the earliest opportunity. The UK has never taken a leading role and the British people have never displayed much enthusiasm for the project. In Britain only two front rank politicians, the former Tory Prime Minister Ted Heath and the former Labour Chancellor Lord Jenkins, have ever openly embraced European integration.

The assumption in the late 1990s is that the British public is opposed to European Economic and Monetary Union because that is what the polls show and that is what most newspapers say. This is one of the reasons for Labour's caution over EMU, since their election to government in 1997. However, this may be a case of the leaders following what they believe to be public opinion when in fact that opinion may be fluid. It may be that on issues such as this, the public would respond to strong leadership, so that if, for example, politicians such as the current Prime Minister, Tony Blair, the Chancellor, Gordon Brown, the former Conservative Chancellor, Kenneth Clarke and the former Conservative Deputy Prime Minister, Michael Heseltine campaigned *for* the EMU, the public would follow, especially if the newspapers threw their weight behind it. It is often said that the Murdoch press is irretrievably hostile towards EMU; but the same was said about their relationship with the Labour Party, and yet in the 1997 election, *The Sun* endorsed Tony Blair. Partly this was because *The Sun*'s readership supported Tony Blair, and like any good businessman, Rupert Murdoch did not want to be too far out of line with his customers. The same could happen over Europe.

SUMMARY

This study diagram attempts to put the institutions and the concepts together:

Table 1: *Summary*		
KEY CONCEPTS	ORGANISING PRINCIPLE	EU INSTITUTIONS
Supranationalism	Federalism	European Parliament $+\mathcal{BANK}$ European Commission European Court of Justice
Intergovernmentalism	Functionalism	Council of Ministers European Council

STUDY GUIDES

Revision hints

You will be returning to much of the material discussed in this first chapter. Your notes need only be brief but it is important that you understand:

1 the debate within the United Kingdom and elsewhere, about the nature of the European Union, the kind of organisation it is and might become, especially the distinction between intergovernmental and supranational, and the nature of federalism;

2 the roles played within the European Union by the different institutions (Parliament, Council of Ministers, Commission and Court) and the way in which each of these is related to the two guiding principles of the European Union as it has developed, intergovernmentalism and supranationalism.

Exam hints

Stephen George has described the United Kingdom as 'an awkward partner' in European terms. He is careful to stress that she is *an* awkward state rather than *the* awkward one; France, Denmark and Greece in their different ways can all be said to have been awkward over the years. However there does seem to be some sense in which the United Kingdom is set apart from the Continent, and not just geographically. Before embarking on a detailed look at the history and politics of the British relationship with Europe, it would be worth thinking about the roots of this difference.

Consider the following essay titles:

1   'Somewhere Between An Obligation and a Mistake'. Comment on this view of British attitudes towards membership of the European Union.

2   'The British people have never really been asked for their views on European integration which is why they have always seen it as something imposed upon them'. Discuss.

Both questions are concerned with the relationship that the British people, rather than the political and economic elites, have had with Europe. The implication of both (although clearly you are not forced to agree with it) is that British opinion has been at best apathetic and acquiescent to Europe, and at worst positively hostile. To address the truth of these claims, you need to think about the way in which decisions about Britain's role within Europe have been taken. This will not need the detailed historical material from subsequent chapters; you simply need to think about and discuss the ways in which decisions on entry were taken by the elite, and then presented as involving largely economic implications rather than having any great bearing on sovereignty.

These essays are 'macro' in the sense that they involve a broad brush approach, outlining the arguments in a general way rather than going into any great detail about particular institutions or particular policies. Later on when we have considered the issues in more detail, it would be useful to look again at the arguments implicit in these essay titles, but for now, treat them as introductory.

Practice Questions

1   Is it fair to describe the UK as 'an awkward partner' in relation to Europe?
2   'The European issue is so important to the UK that it should be at the top of the political agenda.' Discuss.

2

BRITAIN AND EUROPE
1945 TO 1973

Introduction

THIS CHAPTER CONSIDERS the historical background to British entry to the European Union, so that we have a context within which to evaluate the experience of membership. We need to consider why the UK did not wish to be part of the European project when the other countries of Europe wanted her involved, and why, by the time the UK had changed her mind, France did not want her involved. The history of the relationship between the emerging Community and the UK is revealed as cautious and suspicious. It is necessary to look briefly at that history in order to understand the impact that Europe has had upon the British political system.

The British preference has always been for intergovermentalism as opposed to supranationalism, and in this they have often been supported by France; Germany and the Benelux states (Belgium, Netherlands and Luxembourg) have tended to favour supranationalism, leading to a federal Europe.

Key Points

This chapter looks at the following issues:

* Why European states began to integrate after the Second World War.
* The attitude of the UK to such developments.
* The reasons behind the UK's changed decision.
* The divisions within the British political elites over the European issue.

THE BRITISH SAY 'NON MERCI'

In June 1947, the US Secretary of State George Marshall offered American aid to war-torn Europe. He made it clear that US aid was dependent on greater European cooperation; the European governments had to consult and cooperate together to decide their needs and collectively deal with the USA. The Labour Party was in government in the UK, and Foreign Secretary, Ernest Bevin, saw to it that, as demanded by the USA, aid was channelled through the Organisation for European Economic Cooperation (an 18-member body that included France, Italy and the Benelux states established in April 1948, in which decision-taking was by unanimous vote, not by majority). This type of *intergovernmental* arrangement suited the British government because it involved no loss of sovereignty; each state could veto decisions if it felt it necessary.

However, *federalist* thinking lay behind the creation of the Council of Europe. In a speech in Zurich in 1946, the Conservative Party Leader and former Prime Minister, Winston Churchill stated that

> *'if Europe were once united in the sharing of its common inheritance, there would be no limits to the happiness of, to the prosperity and glory which its three or four hundred million people would enjoy'.*

He seemed to be calling for a United States of Europe. Inspired by this speech European federalists, such as Paul Henri Spaak from Belgium, and Italy's De Gougeri, called a Congress of Europe in May 1948. It established the European Movement, which created the Council of Europe in May 1949. When the Council tried to promote federalism through a Consultative Assembly, the plan met British objections. Britain would only agree to an organisation dominated by an intergovernmental Committee of Ministers.

The Assembly does exist, indeed it is the widest parliamentary forum in Europe but it does not possess legislative powers. The most important achievement of the Council of Europe was the **Convention on Human Rights** in 1950. The UK is a signatory to this document, indeed British lawyers played an important part in drafting it, and the UK was the first country to ratify it in March 1951.

However both the Labour government of 1945–1951 and the Conservative Party made it clear that Britain had no intention of joining any kind of supranational organisation in which the wishes of nation states could be overridden. Labour believed that any European organisation would be dominated by Christian Democrats (European Conservatives) and would prevent public ownership. Britain did not therefore welcome another development, the plan for a European Coal and Steel Community.

THE EUROPEAN COAL AND STEEL COMMUNITY

In 1950 the French Foreign Secretary, Robert Schuman, proposed a pooling of the French and German coal and steel industries of the Ruhr and the Saar regions. Since the defeat of Germany in 1945, these industries had been under the control of the International Ruhr Authority. The French were anxious to continue to keep West German coal and steel under international supervision when this body was wound up. Other countries were invited to join the European Coal and Steel Community (ECSC) and four did so: Belgium, Holland, Luxembourg and Italy.

The ECSC was largely the creation of the French federalist Jean Monnet. To Bevin's annoyance, the American government was told about the plan before the British. A Labour Cabinet Minister Herbert Morrisson commented that Britain could not take part because 'the Durham miners won't wear it'. Monnet was not prepared to let British objections block the scheme; he wrote to the then British Chancellor Stafford Cripps,

> *'I hope with all my heart that you will join in this from the start. But if you do not we shall go ahead without you.'*

THE TREATY OF PARIS 1951

This Treaty established the setting up of the ECSC. But, the aim was more than simply economic cooperation; it was also intended to prevent any future conflict between France and Germany. The preamble to the Treaty states that the aim was

> *'to establish ... the foundation of a broad and independent community among peoples long divided by bloody conflicts; and to lay the basis of institutions capable of giving direction to their future common destiny'.*

These were the main features of the Treaty:

- The ECSC had a supranational High Authority; members operated free of national interest and made decisions on the principle of majority voting. A Court of Justice was set up independently of member governments to adjudicate on actions of the High Authority and ensure that the Treaty was enforced.
- A Council of Ministers with one representative from each member government would make decisions based on proposals from the High Authority.
- A Common Assembly would have advisory but not legislative functions.

This structure was to form the institutional basis for the EEC when it was created in 1957, and in many ways it is still the basis of the European Union in the late 1990s.

THE COMMON MARKET AND THE TREATIES OF ROME 1957

In June 1955 the ECSC Ministers met at Messina, Italy, to consider the creation of a customs union and a community for the pooling of atomic energy. The aim of Euratom, as envisioned by the governments involved in the ECSC, was to promote cooperation in the new energy source and make sure that research was done on a Community rather than a national basis. Anthony Eden had been elected Prime Minister of the Conservative Government in May 1955, but British policy did not change. The government sent only a civil servant to Messina as an observer, and he was soon withdrawn.

In March 1957 with full backing from the USA, the two Treaties of Rome set up the European Economic Community and Euratom. They were ratified by the six governments (France, Germany, Italy, the Benelux countries) and came into effect in January 1958. The implementation of the goals outlined in the EEC would create a Common Market. Every effort was made to involve the UK. However, the British government decided to stay out because the structures of the British economy were so different to those on the Continent, particularly:

- the role of agriculture
- the role of sterling
- the Commonwealth markets.

At that stage, the British economy was larger than that of either West Germany or France.

Summary

So, Labour had turned down the opportunity to join the ECSC in 1950, and the Conservatives turned down the invitation to join the Common Market in 1955. The British policy-makers of the 1940s and 1950s, the likes of Winston Churchill, Clement Attlee, Ernest Bevin and Anthony Eden, were born in the late nineteenth century and had grown up in a world in which the British Empire was truly global. The UK was the only combatant to fight both world wars from start to finish. It is surely understandable that such men would find it very hard to accept that the UK should surrender sovereignty to a continental organisation, the members of which had either recently been enemies of their country, or had been occupied by Nazi Germany.

Although the UK had emerged victorious from the Second World War, her economy had been put under enormous strain. By 1945, the UK was clearly in third place militarily, behind the two superpowers, the USSR and the USA. Yet British politicians of all parties believed that the country should continue to be a great power. Churchill argued that the UK was in a unique position at the centre of three concentric circles, representing:

1 her Empire (soon to be turned into a Commonwealth)
2 her 'special' relationship with the USA
3 her role in Europe.

As he put it in the Commons in 1953 'we are *with* but not *of* Europe'.

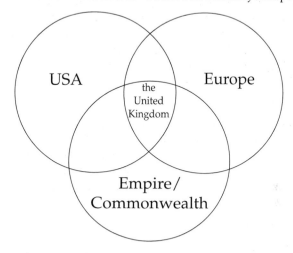

The economic historian Alan Milward argues that 'failure to sign the Treaties of Rome was a serious mistake', based on the mistaken belief that the UK was 'still in some sense a great power whose foreign policy should reflect that position'. Stephen George agrees, arguing that the withdrawal from Messina was 'possibly the biggest tactical mistake that Britain made in its attempt to create the sort of Europe that it preferred'. The British were putting political calculations before economic ones.

HUMILIATION OVER THE SUEZ CRISIS

The Suez Crisis of 1956 – the UK colluded with France and Israel in an attempt to overthrow the Egyptian leader General Abdul Nasser – revealed the limitations of British power. Nasser had nationalised the Suez Canal, which was built by French engineers in 1869 and, as much of the shipping passing through Suez was British and the Canal linked the Mediterranean to the Red Sea, had always been of great commercial and strategic importance to the British. The Labour Party under Hugh Gaitskell opposed Eden's operation, but more importantly the American President Dwight Eisenhower and his Secretary of State John Foster Dulles were against it and gave Britain an ultimatum: either arrange a cease-fire between the British and Egyptian forces or face the financial consequences of a withdrawal of US economic support.

The two world wars had weakened the British economy to such an extent that it could not survive without US assistance. In the face of the US ultimatum, Britain immediately drew back from Egypt to the dismay of the French, who saw it as typical of Britain's subordination to the USA. Six months after the Suez crisis, the French National Assembly (which had killed off the idea for a European Defence Community) ratified the Treaty of Rome because by creating a stronger and therefore potentially more autonomous Western Europe it would secure independence from both the USA and the USSR.

The Suez crisis led to Prime Minister Anthony Eden's resignation in January 1957. The new Conservative Prime Minister Harold Macmillan, gave priority to rebuilding good relations with America. The British hoped to create a free trade zone to include the UK, the EEC and any other Western European countries which wished to join. Macmillan hoped that when exposed to a vast free trade area, the Community would 'melt like a lump of sugar in a cup of tea'. The French vetoed the British idea, so instead the British took the lead in creating the European Free Trade Association (EFTA) in 1959. Aimed at removing tariffs on industrial goods by 1970 and comprising Austria, Denmark, Norway, Portugal, Sweden, Switzerland and the UK, this was purely a free trade area which did not impinge on the sovereignty of Parliament.

THE BRITISH CHANGE THEIR MIND

An alliance of British industry, the financial interests of the City of London, the Foreign Office and the American government persuaded Harold Macmillan to reverse policy over Europe. The arguments in favour of membership were largely economic; the age of imperial preference was over, and the UK was trading more with Europe than with the Commonwealth. The economies of the Continent, particularly West Germany and France, were growing more rapidly than the British – they appeared to be enjoying economic miracles while the British were suffering relative decline.

In 1957, two British colonies Malaya and Ghana were made independent. By 1961 the British Empire was rapidly being dismantled, with Macmillan talking of a 'wind of change' sweeping white minority rule out of the continent of Africa. As a former US Secretary of State Dean Acheson said, 'Britain had lost an Empire and had yet to find a role'. President J.F. Kennedy, believing a more prosperous Western Europe would complement NATO, the Western defence organisation, (at their meeting in April 1961) encouraged Macmillan to apply to the EEC for membership.

Winston Churchill had seen the UK as at the centre of three concentric circles – Empire, the special relationship with the USA and Europe. Now the Empire was being dismantled and the Americans wanted the UK to join the European Economic Community.

THE FIRST APPLICATION TO JOIN – 1961

After over a decade in power, the Conservatives needed a policy that would appear modern and fresh, and Harold Macmillan believed that Europe would reap electoral dividends for his party. The Deputy Leader, R.A. Butler, warned Macmillan that the issue could split the party: 'we might share the fate of Peel and his supporters'. (Robert Peel had split the Conservative Party in 1846 when he repealed the Corn Laws which had protected British agriculture, in order to promote free trade.) It was only the French President De Gaulle's veto against British membership that saved Macmillan from confrontation with the imperialist wing of his party. De Gaulle had come to power in the crisis of 1958, as the French Fifth Republic was set up. Having observed British behaviour in the Suez affair, he believed that the UK would be too much of a 'Trojan horse' for the Americans. Delivered at a press conference, his decision was unilateral and came as a shock to the other member states.

The Labour Party was also divided over Europe. The Labour Leader, Hugh Gaitskell, opposed entry to the EEC. He was on the right of the party, but on this issue he alienated his usual rightwing allies such as Roy Jenkins, Tony Crosland and George Brown, and pleased the anti-EEC leftwingers such as the then rebel backbencher, Michael Foot.

THE SECOND ATTEMPT

France was the dominant force within the Community from its creation until the late 1970s, when the German currency became the basis of the European Monetary System. De Gaulle controlled France from 1958 to 1969 during which time he pushed the Community in the direction he wanted. In 1962 the Common Agricultural Policy was created, to the advantage of French farmers. (The result has been that agricultural prices and the incomes of farmers have been left not to the market place, but to the European authorities.)

In August 1965, the Euratom and the EEC were merged in a Treaty, thereby creating the European Communities. French objections to various proposals, particularly over the financing of the Common Agricultural Policy, and of the ambitions of the German President of the Commission, Walter Hallstein, meant that from July 1965, France boycotted meetings of the Council of Ministers. The impasse was resolved by the Luxembourg Compromise of January 1966 which agreed that unanimous voting would be the norm at the Council of Ministers. This contradicted the Treaty of Rome, but reflected De Gaulle's belief in intergovernmentalism. Ironically it would mean that the Community which the UK joined in 1973 was operating much more in line with the inter-governmentalist sympathies of the British than the supranationalist ambitions of the federalist Charles Monnet.

The Labour Party's 1966 general election manifesto said that a Labour government would support entry only on the right terms. By 1967, the Labour government under Harold Wilson applied to join the Community, again partly for electoral reasons. The application was likely to meet the same rebuff as the Tories faced six years earlier, but as Labour's pro-Europe policy would prevent the Conservatives from monopolising the stance, it removed a distinctive issue from the new Tory leader Heath. Sure enough French President De Gaulle vetoed the application.

THIRD TIME LUCKY

President De Gaulle lost office in 1969 and died shortly afterwards. Although the new French President George Pompidou also had reservations about British membership, the crucial decision to open negotiations with the UK was taken by the leaders of the six member states at the Hague Summit of 1969. In June 1970, Labour unexpectedly lost office to the Conservatives under Edward Heath, who managed to do what Harold Macmillan and Harold Wilson had failed to accomplish, to take the UK into the Common Market. The 1970 Conservative manifesto had said that there would need to be 'the full hearted consent of the people'. Douglas Hurd (then Edward Heath's assistant, who later became Foreign Secretary under Margaret Thatcher and John Major) was the author of that famous phrase about 'consent', a phrase that would come back to haunt the Conservatives.

Harold Wilson claimed that the terms which Edward Heath had accepted were unreasonable to the UK, and therefore the official Labour line was to oppose entry. However in November 1971, 69 Labour MPs, some of them from the highest reaches of the party, rebelled against a three line whip and voted with the Conservative government. This led to a 356–244 vote in favour of membership of the EEC. Thirty-nine Tory MPs had voted against, so in Martin Holmes's words, 'having failed to convince his own party, Heath was bailed out by Labour rebels'.

The necessary legislation was completed in 1972, and on 1st January 1973, the United Kingdom, together with two other new members, Denmark and the Republic of Ireland, formally joined the European Community; this was 16 years after the Treaty of Rome, and 10 years after Charles De Gaulle's first rebuff. It was arguably the most profound change to the constitution, economy and political system of the United Kingdom since the introduction of democracy.

SUMMARY

It is useful to put the issues which led the UK to change her mind into diagrammatic form. The diagram attempts to illustrate the multiple influences which led the British to change their mind about European integration. The awareness of relative economic decline is apparent from comments made by politicians at the time. American pressure was especially strong when J.F. Kennedy became President. EFTA had been formed in 1960, but had clearly failed in the sense that it was a very limited free trade arrangement, and had not delivered a major boost to the British economy. The dismantling of Empire, whether speeded up by Suez or not, was evidence that Britain's influence globally was contracting. Relative economic decline had provoked a desire to modernise the British economy and with it British society, which was increasingly seen as trapped in outdated assumptions revealed in class differences. Finally elite pressure groups such as business were lobbying for a change of policy towards Europe.

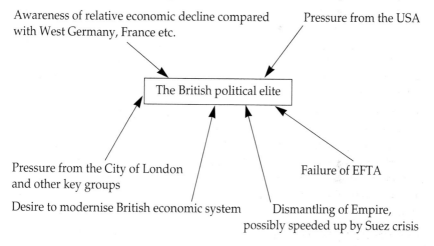

Awareness of relative economic decline compared with West Germany, France etc.

Pressure from the USA

The British political elite

Pressure from the City of London and other key groups

Failure of EFTA

Desire to modernise British economic system

Dismantling of Empire, possibly speeded up by Suez crisis

It is not necessary to have detailed historical knowledge of the different moves towards European integration but it is useful to consider the extent to which progress in one area, for example over coal and steel, 'spiltover' into movement in another area, for example, defence, and so on. To this end it is useful to put the issues into diagrammatical form in order to see the linkages between the ECSC, the EDC, the EEC and Euratom. *Note*: the OEEC changed into the OECD in 1961 when it expanded to include the major non-European capitalist powers.

Table 2: *Summary*		
INSTITUTIONS INVOLVING THE UK	PROPOSALS WHICH 'FAILED' TO BE ADOPTED	INSTITUTIONS EXCLUDING THE UK
The OECD	The EDC	The ECSC
The Council of Europe		The EEC
NATO Western European Union		Euratom

STUDY GUIDES

Revision Hints

Your notes need to enable you to understand firstly, why certain European states, in particular France and West Germany, wanted to integrate their economic and political systems in the aftermath of the Second World War, and secondly, why most British politicians, of all major parties, at first felt that it was not necessary or appropriate for the UK to join such a process. It is vital to have this historical background clear, because it affects the debate about whether the UK missed an opportunity to join the organisation before the rules were drawn up, so that the UK could possibly have influenced those rules more to her own advantage; it also provokes questions about the continued difficulties which the United Kingdom has with the rest of the European Union.

You need a full set of notes on the second part of the chapter, because it marks the turning point in the UK's relations with Europe. You could draw up a time line so that you are clear about the sequence of events. It is also worth organising the notes *thematically*:

- What were the economic reasons for the UK changing her mind?
- What were the domestic political reasons behind the change?
- What about her relationship with the Commonwealth?
- What about the role of the United States?

1 'The UK did not join the European Community because it felt that it was historically separate from Europe'. Discuss.

2 Would the UK have been less of an awkward partner in Europe if she had joined the Community at the outset?

The first question invites you to consider what was it that made the British feel 'separate' from Europe, and to what extent were such feelings justified. This requires examination of the British experience of world war, her Empire and her supposed special relationship with the United States. In no case is it necessary to go into great historical detail, but it is essential to appreciate the impact that such experiences and attitudes had on the British mentality. The UK was the only state to fight both world wars from first to last, and in both cases she came out on the 'winning side'. This was bound to colour attitudes towards her postwar development. It could be argued that failure to join was the product of a desire to separate the UK from Europe, to emphasise British exceptionalism.

The second essay is concerned with the extent to which the absence of the UK from the early moves towards integration meant that the rules of the Community were shaped in the interests of other states, particularly West Germany and France. The result is that by the time the UK did join, then policies such as CAP were well established and appeared to work against British interests. There is also the point that the time when the UK was not a member was the time of greatest economic growth within the Community. On the other hand it could be argued that British 'awkwardness' is a product of a very different political culture and structure of government, such that entry at whatever moment would not have affected the sense that the UK is an 'outsider' alongside continental states.

Practice Questions

1 Why did it take so long for the UK to join the European Community?
2 'By the time the UK had joined the European Community the rules had already been shaped to suit others.' Discuss the validity of this statement.

3

THE IMPACT OF MEMBERSHIP ON THE BRITISH ECONOMY

Introduction

THIS CHAPTER LOOKS at the **political economy** of the European Union. Although the UK became a member of the Community in 1973, it was only really in the late 1980s and 1990s that the implications of British membership of the European Union came to the centre of the British political stage. The debates about the Exchange Rate Mechanism, the Single Market, the Maastricht Treaty and Economic Monetary Union cover important aspects of political economy, because they are economic issues with huge implications for politics, rather than simply technical matters of economics.

Key Points

This chapter contains material on the following key issues:

- The economic relationship between the UK and the European Union.
- The argument over the UK's contributions to the European Budget, and the importance of the Single European Act, 1986.
- The debate over the Exchange Rate Mechanism and the nature of Britain's involvement in it.
- The various issues surrounding Economic and Monetary Union.

ECONOMIC RELATIONS BETWEEN THE UK AND THE EU

British membership of the EEC took effect in 1973 just as the long postwar economic boom based on a system of fixed exchange rates and American domination of the global economy, was beginning to unravel. The costs of the Vietnam War which had begun in 1965, weakened the US dollar, which in turn weakened sterling. Commodity prices were rising rapidly, and the Arab/Israeli crisis in October 1973 which quadrupled the price of oil, ushered in the energy shortage and a period of galloping inflation. By 1975 inflation in the UK had reached a peacetime high of around 25 per cent.

Thus the British entry into the European Community coincided with the end of the age of affluence, and the onset of an age of austerity. Of course it is possible that the British economy would have been in an even worse condition had the country stayed out of the Community. Even so it meant that disillusion with Europe rapidly set in because the British had been 'sold' the idea of the Community as economically advantageous. Had the UK joined in 1957 when the European economy was booming, perhaps the public would have seen it in a more positive light; as it was, there was much grudging talk about the economic costs of membership.

By 1995, the British contribution to the EU was £7 billion, about 2 per cent of government spending, out of a total EU budget of £67 billion. The EU spent about £4 billion on the UK through the Common Agricultural Policy (CAP) and aid to the poorest regions of the UK such as Northern Ireland and Merseyside. The EU's total economic output (the equivalent of a nation's Gross National Product) of about 6 trillion dollars compares with 5 trillion for the USA and three trillion for Japan. In October 1991 the European Free Trade Association (EFTA) agreed with the European Community the creation of the **European Economic Area**, the largest free trade zone in the world.

The former British Ambassador to France, Nicholas Henderson, points out that in the late 1990s, around 60 per cent of British trade is with the EU countries. More British goods are bought by Germany than by the USA, more by Sweden (a member of the EU since 1995) than the whole of Latin America, and more by Ireland than by Canada, South Africa, Australia and New Zealand combined.

However the sheer magnitude of British trade with fellow EU members does not necessarily mean that it has been to Britain's advantage. Sceptics argue that the figure of 60 per cent is used to disguise the fact that the UK has a chronic trade deficit with the EU. Before entry in 1973, the UK purchased wheat from North America and butter from New Zealand at world prices; after entry it was forced to switch to more expensive European sources. It was this which provoked the rows over Britain's budget contributions.

THE BUDGETARY ISSUE

By 1979, the British found that their net contribution to the EC budget was the second highest of all member states, despite the fact that the British economy was not as successful as most of those states. This was because the bulk of EC spending was on agriculture, and the UK has a relatively small and highly efficient agricultural sector. A temporary accommodation was reached in 1980 but the underlying grievance remained. At that stage, pre-QMV (qualitative majority voting), any member state was able to veto decisions, and Britain made it clear at the Athens summit of 1983 that it was prepared to do so if Britain did not get a satisfactory conclusion to her budget dilemma.

Having served as President of the European Commission from 1977 to 1981, the former Labour politician Roy Jenkins records in his diaries how Margaret Thatcher as Prime Minister made such an issue of Britain's budgetary contributions, that while she may well have achieved a reduction in Britain's payments by 1984, it was at the cost of alienating other European leaders such as French President François Mitterand, Helmut Schmidt and German Chancellor Helmut Kohl, who at one point in 1984 walked out of the negotiations.

The **Fontainbleu Agreement** of June 1984 marked the final resolution of the budgetary issue. Britain was to receive a rebate of two-thirds of the difference between its receipts from and payment into the EU budget. New bones of contention rapidly appeared; according to Alan Watson, 'far from settling [Margaret] Thatcher's alleged anti-Europeanism, the budget settlement seemed only to encourage it'.

THE SINGLE EUROPEAN ACT, 1986

By the mid 1980s the Eurosclerosis (a term coined by the pro-free trade British magazine *The Economist* meaning stagnation) which had bedevilled the EC since the early 1970s, was giving way to a new era of dynamism. In 1981 the **Genscher-Colombo** initiative, an attempt on the part of the West German Foreign Secretary and his Italian counterpart to promote further integration, came to little, but the Stuttgart heads of government meeting of December 1983 restated the central objective of the Treaty of Rome – 'an ever closer union between the peoples of Europe'. At the same time as the British Labour Party was suffering its landslide defeat at the hands of Thatcherism in 1983, the French Socialists under François Mitterand were abandoning the brief experiment with Keynesianism. (John Maynard Keynes was a British economist who argued that governments can manage demand in such a way as to avoid mass unemployment, if they are willing to spend money during recessions.)

François Mitterand had been elected to the French Presidency in 1981 on a leftwing programme and had attempted to implement it. However, with Thatcherism triumphant in Britain, American President Ronald Reagan pursuing very similar policies in the USA, and a shift to the right in Germany with the formation of the Kohl government in 1982, the French were out on a limb. The French Finance Minister Jacques Delors persuaded Mitterand that France had to return to orthodox financial discipline, which it did by 1983. In 1985, Delors took over the Presidency of the Community. With these three figures in effective control of the Community, Helmut Kohl (Chancellor from 1982), François Mitterand (President from 1981 to 1995) and Jacques Delors (President of the Commission from 1985 to 1994), Europe moved in the direction that France and Germany wanted and the UK had almost always opposed – 'ever closer union'.

Tariffs and quota restrictions within the Community had been abolished in 1968 with completion of the customs union, but economic integration was far from being achieved. A *common* market had to give way to a *single* market of 320 million people, otherwise Europe would not be able to compete with the USA, Japan or the newly industrialising countries, the Far East Asian 'tigers' economies. June 1985 saw the publication by the Commission of a White Paper, *Completing the Internal Market*, which was approved by the Milan meeting of the European Council at the end of that month. The author was Lord Cockfield, an EC Commissioner and former Minister of Trade under Margaret Thatcher, thus it was the product of the French Socialist Delors and a British Conservative. Delors saw it as cover for his real aim – political union. In December 1985, the Luxembourg European Council (Prime Ministers and Heads of State) agreed the principles which were written into the Single European Act (SEA) which was adopted by all national legislatures in 1986.

The SEA was signed in February 1986, to come into effect in July 1987. It sought to move from a common market to a single market, and in so doing galvanised the Community after a decade of lethargy. The programme involved 300 measures to remove no-tariff barriers, physical, technical and fiscal, with each item having to be agreed by the Council of Ministers but on the basis of QMV. The aim was completion of the internal market by 1992.

This Act was a diluted version of the European Parliament's proposal for a Treaty of Union based on the Spinelli Report of 1984, but even so it marked the first comprehensive reform of EC treaties. Altiero Spinelli, a veteran Italian federalist and MEP, had persuaded President Mitterand of the need for revival of the European idea and this became the defining idea of Mitterand's Presidency. The SEA amended the Treaty of Rome and introduced important institutional changes such as more power to the European Parliament and more use of Qualitative Majority Voting, but because it was the product of the free market thinking which was very much in the ascendancy in the mid 1980s, it was welcomed by Thatcherites in the UK. They believed that deregulation of financial markets would lead to huge gains for British banks and insurance companies. In Anderton's words

> '[Margaret Thatcher] believed the SEA would repeat and extend the deregulated internal market she championed in the UK, only to discover it leading towards the single currency she detested.'

Labour voted against it on second reading, but the government forced it through the Commons by cutting short the debate – a guillotine; in the words of the then Labour MP Peter Shore, 'one of the most profoundly anti-democratic acts in parliamentary history.'

In her memoirs, Margaret Thatcher talks of the acrimonious Milan summit of 1985 which ensured the inclusion of Qualitative Majority Voting in the SEA.

> 'To my astonishment and anger Signor Craxi suddenly called a vote and by a majority the council resolved to establish an Inter-Governmental Conference'.

In the debate over the Maastricht Treaty in July 1993 (by which time John Major was Prime Minister), Margaret Thatcher claimed that the Commission had interpreted its powers under the SEA much further than was 'understood' when she signed the 1986 Treaty. She had agreed to the majority voting principle in the SEA not knowing that 'Brussels would abuse these powers'.

Peter Shore argues that

> 'by agreeing to its preface which commits Europe 'to transform relations as a whole among their states into a European union' Thatcher can truly be said to have been, if not the mother, then at least the midwife to the Maastricht process.'

The moral of the story is that although European Treaties may be dull, their detail is important and may come back to vex politicians long after they have been agreed. Thatcher subsequently refused to renew Lord Cockfield's appointment as EC Commissioner, claiming that he had 'gone native', ie, sided with the majority of EC countries. He was replaced by Leon Brittan who had resigned from the Thatcher government in January 1986 over the Westland crisis (see p. 72).

The SEA was supposed to help realise the four freedoms – free movement of:

* persons
* goods
* services
* capital.

A report at the time by an Italian economist, Cecchini, claimed that the SEA would increase Europe's GDP by 4.25–6.5 per cent. However by early 1997, studies by the Commission showed that GDP was only 1.5 per cent higher than it would have been without the SEA. The single-market commissioner, Mario Monti, argues that the shortfall was due to German reunification in 1990 and the subsequent recession. Even so Monti describes the SEA as 'the largest supply side operation in history'. *The Economist* pointed out that the movement to eliminate all barriers to a single market by December 31st 1992 'has focused attention on the ultimate barrier to a single market, the lack of a single currency'.

THE EXCHANGE RATE MECHANISM

Fluctuation in the exchange rate has caused a variety of problems for the British economy. The Conservative government under Ted Heath 'floated' the pound sterling in 1972. This consisted of leaving the exchange rate to move up or down according to the valuation of the market. Having only been worth about $1.50 in 1976, the pound went up to $2.40 by 1980 as high interest rates, the effect of North Sea oil (which turned the pound into a 'petrocurrency') and the markets' enthusiasm for Thatcherism all increased demand for sterling. The Confederation of British Industry (CBI) and the Trade Union Conference (TUC) complained that the overvalued pound was hurting British manufacturing, and indeed, a deep industrial recession followed. In contrast, by January 1985, the US dollar reached new heights as the pound fell to a historic low of $1.03. The volume of British exports went up but so did the price of imports. Measured against the deutsch mark, the pound had fallen from about 8 in 1971, to 4.5 in 1981, to below 3 by 1986.

Such fluctuations make it very difficult for business, particularly those that export, to plan ahead. They cannot know what their products will cost abroad and therefore cannot estimate demand or plan supply. At the same time they cannot know what effect the exchange rate will have on the price of imports.

Europe's leaders had discussed some form of monetary union since the late 1960s when the whole postwar system of fixed exchange rates began to crack. The Labour government devalued the pound in 1967, but more importantly the American dollar, the basis of the capitalist order, was weakening. However, any attempt at monetary union was derailed by the economic collapse of the early 1970s, and it was not until the end of the decade before any real progress was made. The ERM had been set up in 1978 just before Margaret Thatcher came to power in the UK. It was dominated by the deutsch mark, the only currency never to be devalued within it. It was created outside the framework of the European Community (not all member states participated) by French and German pressure and against resistance from some in the Commission, although not the President Roy Jenkins.

Both Margaret Thatcher and her immediate predecessor as PM, James Callaghan believed that sterling was not ready to join the ERM. Thatcher stuck to her negative view of the ERM, indeed she is reported to have vetoed formal discussion of British membership of the ERM so that the Cabinet was unable to consider the issue. In her view the exchange rate should be left to market forces, and membership of the ERM involved a surrender of power over crucial economic issues.

The Conservatives won the June 1987 election comfortably enough with European integration not really an issue. However, within a few months of victory the conflict between Number 10 and Number 11 Downing Street over the exchange rate broke openly with Mrs Thatcher famously declaring that 'you cannot buck the market' whilst her Chancellor Nigel Lawson was shadowing the deutsch mark in an attempt to prevent overvaluation of the pound. He had cut taxes in the 1987 budget, a conventional response with an election looming. More controversially he cut them again, drastically, in the 1988 budget. At a time when the economy was already overheating, he cut the top rate of income tax from 60 per cent to 40 per cent, and the standard rate from 27 per cent to 25 per cent.

Following the Wall Street Crash of October 1987, share prices fell in London. In an attempt to prevent this turning into a rerun of the 1929 crash, Nigel Lawson relaxed monetary policy. Interest rates *fell* to 7.5 per cent by June 1988 as the government shadowed the deutsch mark; this prompted a speculative boom in the property market which itself fed through into a consumer boom as property owners spent part of their new-found wealth. Thus by 1988 there was a relaxed fiscal and monetary stance, both of which caused the economy to expand. The recovery which had begun in 1982 had turned by 1988 into a runaway boom. The result was a trade deficit of around £2 billion a month. By the late summer of 1988 the government slammed on the brakes in the form of interest rate *increases*. They would not raise taxes because that would be contrary to the ideology of the New Right, which dictates that low income taxes are necessary to stimulate enterprise.

In June 1988 the European Council in Hanover established a Committee chaired by President of the Commission, Jacques Delors, to report on the feasibility of economic and monetary union. In April 1989, the Delors Report recommended a three stage programme for transforming the European Monetary System (formed in 1978) into European Monetary Union. As a necessary step, all the currencies needed to join the ERM. It was at this point that Nigel Lawson and the then Foreign Secretary, Geoffrey Howe tried to persuade Margaret Thatcher of the need to join the ERM.

By the autumn of 1989, with inflation at 10 per cent and Margaret Thatcher publicly stating that the position of Nigel Lawson was 'unassailable', she chose to bring Professor Alan Walters back as her personal economics adviser. Walters was a well known opponent of the ERM which he described as a 'half-baked idea', and a critic of Lawson's exchange rate management which he described as 'misguided'; Lawson took his appointment as a personal rebuff and demanded that Mrs Thatcher dismiss him. She refused; consequently, in October 1989 Nigel Lawson, the man she had once described as 'my brilliant Chancellor', resigned. Professor Walters followed suit immediately. In his resignation speech, Lawson argued that 'the successful conduct of economic policy is possible only if there is, and is seen to be, full agreement between the PM and the Chancellor'. He now demanded an independent central bank, along the lines of the German Bundesbank, which would make monetary policy free of political pressure.

Nigel Lawson was replaced as Chancellor by John Major, who had been his deputy at the Treasury until just a few months earlier; Douglas Hurd was moved to the Foreign Office as Foreign Secretary. Hurd was a former diplomat who had worked for Ted Heath's government in the early 1970s, and was seen as much more enthusiastic about Europe than the Prime Minister, Mrs Thatcher.

THE UK ENTERS THE EXCHANGE RATE MECHANISM: OCTOBER 1990

In 1990 the combination of Chancellor John Major and Foreign Secretary Douglas Hurd, backed by the Deputy Prime Minister Geoffrey Howe, finally persuaded Margaret Thatcher that the pound should join the ERM. They were able to do so because Mrs Thatcher was in a weak position; by the spring of 1990 the poll tax was implemented, sparking off riots in the streets, and there were huge Tory losses in local elections. Throughout the summer, John Major talked up the currency with rumours of impending entry into ERM. The conditions which Mrs Thatcher had insisted on in June 1989 were waived. The pound joined the ERM on **October 5th 1990** at a rate of 2.95 DM (deutsch mark), plus or minus 6 per cent, which meant that it could rise to a ceiling of 3.13 DM or fall to a floor of 2.78 DM. Entry occurred during a successful Labour Party Conference and the timing was deliberately designed to take the wind out of Labour's sails.

This was a defining moment for the Conservative Party and the UK, and one whose repercussions have remained controversial to this day. It marked the temporary ascendancy of the pro-European wing within the Conservative Party (an ascendancy confirmed by Mrs Thatcher's removal from office within a few weeks). The Labour Party, the Liberal Party, the TUC, most of the media, the City and other pressure groups supported British entry. This powerful coalition of forces showed how elite institutions had accepted the inevitability and desirability of British integration to Europe.

Some people claimed later on that the pound had gone in at too high a rate. As late as the summer of 1990, the pound had been trading at just 2.7 DM. The British rate of inflation at this stage was 10.9 per cent, twice the EC average of 5.5 per cent, and four times the German rate of 2.6 per cent. This was extremely embarrassing for a government which had prided itself on its strong anti-inflationary stance. In the early years of the Thatcher governments, the chosen instrument for curbing inflation and regulating the economy was control of the money supply as measured by what was called Sterling M3. However, by 1985 Nigel Lawson had abandoned this attempt and was looking for an alternative 'financial discipline'. The ERM was to offer such a discipline; entry marked the end of the experiment with 'monetarism in one country'.

Membership was supposed to help create a 'golden scenario' for the Tories, with lower interest rates leading to recovery from recession in time to win the next election. At first the high interest rates (15 per cent, from autumn 1989 to autumn 1990) only seemed to affect the property market, but by the summer of 1990 the country was in recession. Unemployment started to rise in May 1990 after falling for four years; by October 1991 it was up to 8.5 per cent and rising.

Opponents of the ERM feared that it would make it harder to cut interest rates. In fact, upon entry to the ERM interest rates were immediately reduced by 1 per cent, Mrs Thatcher's pre-condition for entry. The Bank of England took the almost unprecedented step of publicly regretting the 1 per cent cut, arguing that it undermined the determination to adopt a tough anti-inflationary stance.

Chancellor John Major opposed it but Margaret Thatcher insisted. Over the 23 months of British membership, interest rates were to be reduced on nine occasions, by five percentage points in total. Within a year of Britain joining, her interest rate had moved from six points above Germany to a single point.

John Major took over from Margaret Thatcher as Prime Minister in November 1990, but the approach to economic policy did not fundamentally change. This is not surprising, given that Major had been Chancellor since October 1989, and between June 1987–July 1989 he had been Nigel Lawson's deputy at the Treasury. John Major appointed Norman Lamont his Chancellor, and together they continued to implement the neo-liberal policies of the New Right. Deregulation was still seen as the cure to all ills. The Employment Secretary under Margaret Thatcher, Michael Howard, stressed the virtues of flexible labour markets and the government boasted of the inward investment that was coming to the UK because of the reforms to British industrial relations. Intergovernmental Conferences on political, economic and monetary union opened in December 1990 with the British government hesitant about committing itself to any further advance.

THE 1992 GENERAL ELECTION

The Lawson boom had ended by 1989 with high interest rates, a trade deficit and relatively high inflation, and the British economy had gone into recession in 1990, a major factor behind the removal of Prime Minister Thatcher. All the opinion polls showed the Conservative Party to be heading for defeat at the next General

Election. Yet, despite presiding over the worst recession in 60 years, John Major's Conservatives won the election of April 1992. The Conservatives attacked Labour's 'tax bombshell' and argued that if Labour were elected, there would be no economic recovery. All three major parties supported membership of the Exchange Rate Mechanism at the election.

The government duly won a majority of 21, the Conservative's fourth successive election victory. They went on to achieve success in the local elections of May 1992, and in June Britain took over the Presidency of the EU. By then the German Chancellor, Helmut Kohl was losing support in Germany, and it was believed that he might lose the next election due in 1994. In France, President Mitterand was running out of political steam, and was due to retire in 1995. John Major appeared to be in a strong position to challenge for the leadership of the EU. The economic recovery in the UK did in fact get underway, but the fiasco over the ERM fatally undermined John Major's government.

BLACK WEDNESDAY: SEPTEMBER 16TH 1992

- In spring 1992, the Maastricht Treaty was being debated by the politicians of Europe.
- In June, the German Central Bank, the Bundesbank, raised interest rates.
- Market fears over the impending French referendum on the Maastricht Treaty, and the overvaluation of several currencies, led speculators to sell the weaker currencies to buy deutsch marks.
- There were calls to devalue sterling, but these were dismissed as it was felt that devaluation would undermine the fight against inflation. (In retrospect it would have made sense to have had a more general currency revaluation at the time of the Maastricht summit.)
- The Italian lira was devalued on 14th September.
- In the absence of significant cuts in German interest rates, the pressure on the pound continued, and even two interest rate increases on the same day were not enough to save the pound.

On Wednesday September 16th 1992 (Black Wednesday to some, White Wednesday to others), the pound and the lira were driven off the ERM. The Spanish peseta devalued by 7 per cent, but the French franc maintained its value, apparently with the help of the Bundesbank. This resulted in a loss of tens of millions of pounds for the British government. Norman Lamont blamed the Bundesbank under its new Governor Schlesinger for failing to cut German interest rates, but Schlesinger had no power to do that by himself. John Major referred to 'faultlines' within the ERM which caused the collapse of the pound. The economist Gavyn Davies, a close confidante of Tony Blair's, agreed with John Major that Britain's problems had been exacerbated by the strength of Germany's post-unification boom, and the lack of support from the Bundesbank.

The Bundesbank is supposed to be independent, but its policies have corresponded regularly to the needs of Helmut Kohl's party, the Christian Democratic Union. (However, in May 1993 a report rejected the British claim that the system was fundamentally flawed; it just needed to be operated more flexibly.)

The effects of Black Wednesday

British interest rates came back down again as soon as the pound left the mechanism, because they no longer had to be used to defend a particular exchange rate. They were to come down repeatedly over the next few years. There was an effective devaluation of 14 per cent against the deutsch mark by November 1992. This devaluation reduced the price of British exports but meant that the price of imports into Britain went up. However this did not lead to high inflation, because with high unemployment, the economy was operating at well under full capacity at the time. Thus devaluation stimulated export-led growth, while tax increases in the UK prevented consumer spending from getting out of hand.

Every other devaluation this century, in 1931, 1949, 1967 and 1976 had occurred when the Labour Party was in government; this is why Labour had been tagged as the party of the weak pound and inflation, and the Tories had a reputation for financial probity. Black Wednesday destroyed that reputation overnight. Roy Jenkins, who became Labour Chancellor after the devaluation of 1967, said of Black Wednesday that he could never remember a time when Britain was so badly governed.

Paradoxically the very failure of the government policy in September 1992 provided the conditions for subsequent economic success, which is why those who had always opposed ERM talk of White Wednesday. However the public never gave the government credit for prosperity, precisely because it was a product of miscalculation rather than design. In November 1990 Major had stated 'we have set an exchange rate for sterling and I do not anticipate moving outside that range. I am wholly unrepentant about the exchange rate I chose'. Even as late as September 1992 he was saying 'there is going to be no devaluation, no realignment'.

The pro-Conservative newspaper, *The Sunday Times* argued that September 1992 was the moment when John Major's government lost its authority, never to regain it. In August 1992 the Tories had been 4 points ahead of Labour in the polls; by October they were 16 points behind. Most political events, even something as important as the Falklands War, have a relatively short lived impact on the opinion polls. They tend not to be mentioned as reasons for supporting or opposing a party within about a year. The ERM experience was different – respondents were still citing it as a reason for disillusion with the Tories over three years later. Partly this was because it gave a boost to the Eurosceptics, who would cite this crisis to support their anti-European views.

By March 1997, John Major described the events of Black Wednesday as a 'political mistake ... events made a monkey out of us'; but it is important to remember that the recession began before Britain entered the ERM. Indeed the recession was caused by high interest rate policy adopted by Chancellors Nigel Lawson and John Major; in the words of the latter when justifying the policy in October 1989,

---

'Inflation must go. Ending it cannot be painless. The harsh truth is that if it isn't hurting it isn't working'.

This policy was itself a product of the lax monetary and fiscal policies in the late 1980s.

However, anti-ERM commentators would argue:

1 The laxness of Nigel Lawson's monetary policy was a product of his misguided attempt to shadow the deutsch mark.
2 The recession was prolonged by the continuation of relatively high interest rates (10 per cent), a product of misguided desire to keep the UK in the ERM.

Despite pressure to resign, the Chancellor, Norman Lamont remained in office. He subsequently claimed that he had offered his resignation but that John Major had refused it, perhaps because *he* had been the architect of the policy that had collapsed on Black Wednesday. It was later revealed that John Major himself had considered resigning, and had wanted Kenneth Clarke to replace him. The Conservative historian John Barnes speaking in the immediate aftermath of the May 1997 General Election defeat argued that a major contributory factor had been John Major's refusal to dismiss Norman Lamont at that point. Lamont was, however, sacked in May 1993, and became an embittered critic of the Major administration; he argued in his resignation speech that it was 'in office but not in power'.

In his first speech as Conservative Party leader in October 1997, William Hague said that British membership of the ERM had been a mistake, and that it was time to start honestly admitting it. It won one of the loudest cheers of the Party Conference. When the CBI endorsed Labour's stance on British entry into EMU Hague, believing business groups had been wrong before and in his eyes taking the wrong view again, reminded them that they had supported ERM.

ECONOMIC AND MONETARY UNION

The Delors Report produced at the Hanover European Council of 1988 came a year after a British General Election in which the 'issue' of Europe had hardly figured. When the Report came out, it was opposed by a majority of MPs on both sides of the House of Commons, yet by 1991 in the run up to the Maastricht Treaty, Labour specifically supported the goal of a single currency. By then Labour had become more and more enthusiastic about European integration, but for the Conservatives the opposite was true: they were increasingly divided over the issue. When Parliament debated the draft treaty on European Union before the summit, senior Conservatives expressed grave reservations about further integration.

The Maastricht Treaty stated that there would be a 'single and stable' currency creating economic and monetary union. It was this, rather than notions of consultation over foreign and defence policy, or protection of social rights, or institutional reform, which was the core of the Treaty. The Treaty established a European system of central banks which would be independent of their national governments *before* the creation of a single currency, but would then be subordinate to a European Central Bank (ECB). The members of the board of the ECB were to be appointed for eight year terms by the Council of Ministers, but they would not be beholden to any political institutions. The single currency will be the responsibility of the European Central Bank, bound by law to act independently of the member states which retain responsibility for fiscal matters.

The convergence criteria (the requirements each potential state has to satisfy before being allowed to join the EMU) were:

* public debt no higher than 60 per cent of GDP
* budget deficit 3 per cent of GDP
* inflation within 1.5 per cent and interest rates within 2 per cent of the three best performers within the Union.

The criteria would inevitably have a deflationary effect, indeed that was their whole purpose. The European Monetary Institute (EMI) would supervise the gradual introduction of EMU. John Major was willing to consider EMU provided it was not 'imposed'; even though the UK retained an opt-out clause, it signed a Treaty which committed Europe to 'the irrevocable fixing of exchange rates leading to the introduction of a single currency'. The Tory Party was willing to unite behind this position at the 1992 General Election.

MASS UNEMPLOYMENT

The citizens of Europe had seen the postwar, full employment boom of 1948–73 give way to the much more volatile economy of the late 1970s and 1980s. Mass unemployment had returned for the first time since the inter-war era. However it could then be blamed on external forces, such as the rise of competition from Japan and other Asian economies. But in the early 1990s, European leaders appeared to have embraced a policy, deflation, in order to achieve EMU, which was in itself adding to unemployment. For the first time in history, the European idea was becoming associated with self-imposed austerity.

The fact that 18 million Europeans were unemployed, around 10 per cent workforce, and 50 million living in poverty, showed the limitations of integration. Agreement was reached at the Edinburgh Summit of December 1992 on aid for the four poorest states – Greece, Portugal, Spain and Ireland. A European Recovery Programme backed by a new European Investment Fund was intended to reflate the economy. The narrow rejection by Switzerland of the European Economic Area (extending the single market to the EFTA states) in December 1992 shows how divided Europe remained; the optimism of 1991 appeared to be evaporating.

By September 1992, the pound and the lire had been driven out of the ERM, and the chances of the UK adopting EMU were considerably reduced. On August 1st 1993, following a speculative attack on the French franc, the ERM was effectively suspended. This damaged the Franco-German relationship and gave new heart to opponents of EMU, which Lamont described as 'dead, redundant, a bit of a fossil'. The Labour MP Bryan Gould claimed that:

> *'the questions of economic and monetary union, and a single currency have been resolved not by arguments or even by votes, but by events.'*

By September 1993, John Major wrote that the 'plain fact is that EMU is not realisable in present circumstances', while Helmut Kohl and François Mitterand were saying the opposite – Stage 2 of EMU according to the Delors Plan would begin on 1st January 1994.

In order to counteract the deflationary consequences of adoption of the convergence criteria, Jacques Delors planned a reflationary package. In December 1993 he published a White Paper, *Growth, Competitiveness and Employment*, calling for action on the environment, and a social economy. It offered both large scale deregulation to please the right, and public spending to tackle unemployment. He was backed by leftwing Labour figures such as Ken Coates the MEP. However the unemployment summit to discuss the measures led to little, with the Tories predictably leading the opposition to it.

The Delors Plan was a **Keynesian** dream in which an expanded EU budget compensated for the effects of EMU and boosted growth. Such ideas underpinned the postwar consensus in British politics, but had fallen into disfavour by the 1970s. Even the Labour Prime Minister James Callaghan had remarked in 1976 that governments could no longer spend their way out of a recession. By the 1980s, with abolition of exchange controls and globally mobile capital, which meant there would no longer be limits to the amount of money that could be switched from country to country, there was even less chance of Keynesian solutions as the French had discovered in 1983. There was therefore little chance of getting the Delors package implemented.

.U

y 1995 of the Gaullist Jacques Chirac as President of France,
thing that would slow down moves towards EMU, and help
.act, Jacques Chirac embodies the divided mind of the French
elɛ.   .he issue of Europe. In opposition he opposed the social and
economiᴄ   .sequences of the policy of a *franc fort* (the strong franc) which had
led to increased unemployment, but once in power he changed his approach and
embraced them. The earlier of the two dates for EMU, 1997, was abandoned. It
had required that a majority of the EU's 15 members meet the convergence
criteria. EMU would now happen in 1999 when no such majority would be
necessary, and those countries which meet the criteria (other than Denmark and
the UK which have opt-outs) would move automatically to EMU. At the Madrid
summit of December 1995 Helmut Kohl got what he wanted on the issues of the
enlargement of the EU and EMU. January 1999 was confirmed as the starting
date for the new currency, to be called the 'Euro'. Helmut Kohl accepted Jacques
Chirac's interpretation of the EU as

---

*'an original construction neither based on a federal model nor limited to a simple free
trade zone'.*

As the nations of Western Europe prepared to meet the convergence criteria for
EMU, the cuts to public spending at a time of high unemployment provoked
citizens' anger:

- Germany had to cut cash spending for the first time since 1953, and by June
  1996 welfare cuts had led 350,000 demonstrators on to the streets of Bonn, the
  largest protest in post-1945 German history. Chancellor Kohl had promised to
  halve Germany's unemployment by 2000, but as late as April 1997, it stood at
  4.5 million.
- The centre-left coalition running Italy from spring 1996 also had to cut
  spending to get the deficit down, (at 5.9 per cent, it was almost twice the
  Maastricht limit).
- The most difficult decisions came in France which had a deficit of 5 per cent of
  GDP. Spending cuts led to riots in the streets in December 1995. Jacques
  Delors' daughter Martine Aubrey, a leading French Socialist, said it was 'not
  worth breaking the country to acquire EMU'.
- In Spain, with an unemployment rate of 22 per cent almost half those under 24
  were without work.

In November 1995 the German Finance Minister Waigel proposed a Stability Pact
so that once EMU exists, member states would have to follow tight economic
criteria or risk heavy fines.

As the former president of the European Parliament, Klaus Hansch, points ‑
a speech in the early 1990s

> *'there is nothing comparable. Not the Treaty of Rome, not the single market. This is totally different to anything that has happened before because it will have a direct, tangible impact on every individual citizen.'*

Gerhard Schroeder (then the Socialist PM of Lower Saxony, now the Chancellor) argued for postponement of the EMU, but was then punished in the polls for his sceptical stance. By 1997 Germany's high level of unemployment made it less likely that it would get its budget deficit within Maastricht limits, which led to rows between the Bundesbank and the politicians as the latter attempted to manipulate the finances to achieve the Maastricht conditions.

It could be argued that many of the problems faced by the European economies were not directly to do with the Maastricht criteria. *The Economist*, for example, argued consistently that unemployment on the continent was a product of failure to follow the British example and create a more flexible labour market. In this sense what was happening was that the Maastricht Treaty and EMU were being used as scapegoats for the failure to reduce the role of the state in the economy and to reduce labour market rigidities. This is another example of the lack of ideological clarity over the European issue.

THE CONSERVATIVE GOVERNMENT AND EMU

The Conservative Party was, and still is, totally divided over EMU. Some opponents concentrated on economics, and the fact that Britain runs a massive trade deficit with the rest of the EU (in 1990 it was £13 billion a year), while others focus more on the constitution. In the words of the Tory backbencher Bill Cash,

> *'monetary union is political union. The power to issue a currency is the power to tax. It is the centre of gravity and would lead inexorably to a single government and a single parliament. This is the goal for federalists and for Germany. From monetary union, all power will flow to the most dominant economy.'*

While the party was in government, the divisions went all the way up to the Cabinet.

- On February 3rd 1995, John Major told a Conservative Way Forward meeting that 'unless the economic conditions were right, a single currency would tear the European Union apart'.
- His Foreign Secretary Douglas Hurd responded to that 'to say either yes or no now to the option of a single currency which might occur in, say, 1999, would be quixotic and unnecessary'.

nneth Clarke continued to claim that EMU was possible
nion. In a speech to the European Movement on February
ied 'it is a mistake to believe that a monetary union need be a
e road to a federal Europe'.

etary Michael Portillo immediately responded that monetary
constitutional issue'. In a speech in 1994, he claimed 'a single
currenc, ould mean giving up the government of the UK'.

- Treasury Secretary Jonathon Aitken agreed 'I would hesitate for an eternity before I came out and said I would vote for a single currency'.

A Tory truce over Europe was shattered by the then Foreign Secretary Malcolm Rifkind's speech on September 18th 1996 in which he warned that,

---

'if monetary union goes ahead, the EU will be divided into two groups of members for the foreseeable future, regardless of any decision by the UK to participate or not'.

Six Tory elder statesmen including Ted Heath, William Whitelaw and Douglas Hurd wrote,

---

'for us to rule out British membership . . . would be to betray our national interest'.

A few days later, Kenneth Clarke described the British 'traditional business of not being able to make up their minds as pathetic'. He was predictably attacked by the rightwinger, John Redwood, but there were also reports that John Major was exasperated. Nicholas Bonsor, a Junior Minister, publicly denounced the Chancellor, and was then persuaded to apologise. It seemed as though collective responsibility was weakening.

THE LABOUR OPPOSITION AND EMU

The Labour Party has so far downplayed the constitutional implications of EMU. As the then Party leader, Tony Blair said in May 1995 'the ultimate judgement must be an economic one'. However there is still a sizeable section of the party which is not Euroenthusiastic. The former Labour Cabinet Minister Peter Shore, a prominent sceptic, was barred from speaking at the 1996 Labour Conference, but fringe meetings debated 'the insanity of a European single currency'. Tony Blair himself told the Conference 'I will not scrap Britain's veto in Europe'. Of the Eurosceptics in Labour's ranks, some were Keynesians critical of the deflationary bias of the Maastricht Treaty. The former Labour Chancellor Dennis Healey was against EMU happening *at all* in 1999.

In 1996 Denzil Davies and Alan Simpson led a group of 50 Europhobe Labour MPs to call for a People's Europe to campaign against EMU. They wanted to show that the single currency would be run by an undemocratic European

PROTOTYPES FOR THE EURO

Central Bank and would ruin Britain's economy and a future Labour government. The Labour MP for Grimsby, Austin Mitchell believes that Labour 'fell in love with Europe' only because Margaret Thatcher was against it.

'It became the only issue on which we took bold, enthusiastic stands, and defied public opinion in the form of widespread mistrust of the EC'.

(*The New Statesman*, 1995)

He opposed EMU on the grounds that it would increase unemployment and that the Maastricht criteria are monetarist, putting financial criteria above other considerations such as levels of unemployment. If EMU is achieved then in Anderton's phrase 'national macro-economic policy becomes a thing of the past'. The single obligation of the European Central Bank will be price stability. The convergence criteria and the stability pact restrict government's ability to spend, tax and borrow. In his eyes, the Conservative Eurosceptics have got it completely wrong; EMU will not lead to a European Superstate, it will lead to a smaller state along lines propounded by people such as Frederick Hayek, the Nobel prize winning economist much admired by Thatcher.

The Liberal Democrat Party leader Paddy Ashdown had rightly warned the Commons as early as 1991 that economic, monetary and political union 'will alter the British constitution and change the way in which we govern ourselves'. If the German government has its way then EMU will, through the Stability Pact, lead to much greater coordination of fiscal policy as well. Finance Ministers would no longer have the right to set their budget deficits; fines may be imposed if a deficit is too big.

THE 1997 GENERAL ELECTION

It is a truism that no election in the UK is won or lost on a single issue; voters make up their minds on a variety of issues. However, the General Election of May 1st 1997 was the only one in British history in which European issues had the *potential* to play a major part – after all, whichever party won it had to take a crucial decision within months of victory on whether Britain should join EMU. Arguably this is the most important question faced by the nation since it joined the European Community. However even during the election, the leadership of both major parties was determined to keep it low down the agenda. John Major obviously feared that his party's divisions over Europe would be off putting to voters, and Tony Blair wanted the election fought on issues such as Tory tax increases and allegations of sleaze rather than difficult questions about Labour's attitude towards EMU. Only the Eurosceptics, particularly in the Tory camp, wanted Europe to have a high profile during the campaign.

Tory opponents of the Maastricht Treaty and EMU such as John Redwood believed that an anti-EU line would play well with the public, and was the only hope for the party. In many cases their individual election addresses, the equivalent of a candidate's manifesto, committed them to voting against EMU which was of course contrary to the agreed Cabinet line of 'wait and see'. When, about half way through the campaign, the news broke that certain Junior Ministers had done this, John Major decided to address the issue. In dramatic fashion he took personal command over the morning press conference and the evening party political broadcast, and delivered a heartfelt plea for the public to back him in his tactic of not declaring either way on EMU.

The studies of the election appear to show that his tactic worked in the very short term, but by polling day the electorate had returned to their domestic concerns and Labour won a spectacular victory.

THE LABOUR GOVERNMENT AND EMU

All the commentators pointed out that in many ways, the Labour government was similar in its approach to the previous Tory administration. In particular, the Labour Party was adamant that it would make a decision on EMU when the time was right, but that the balance of probability was that sterling would not enter in the first wave in 1999. Labour's Foreign Secretary, Robin Cook, notably more sceptical than the Chancellor, Gordon Brown, stressed in *The New Statesman* in 1996 that Labour was in favour of EMU but not on any terms.

'It can only work if there is real economic convergence among the participating countries ... Unless we get that there has to be a question mark over whether we will be able to give up the right to devalue.'

The Labour position is that if the Cabinet agree to enter and if Parliament approves, it will be put to the people in a referendum. Prime Minister Blair refers to this as a *triple lock*: Cabinet, Parliament, and people all having to approve. However, if collective responsibility holds, then the Cabinet would do what the Prime Minister and Chancellor approve of, and with a majority of 179 in the House of Commons, Parliament also poses no real problems. The real obstacle is winning the referendum in the teeth of apparent public and press hostility.

One of the earliest actions of the new Chancellor was to give the Bank of England operational independence. The government still sets the inflation target and controls the membership of the Board of the Bank. While not going as far to creating a truly independent central bank as some wanted, this does mean that interest rates are raised or lowered by the Bank for economic reasons rather than by the Chancellor for political ones. The Bank still had to work within criteria set by the Chancellor, but this step had paved the way for British membership of EMU.

By the autumn of 1997, the markets were increasingly sensitive to rumours about the government's approach to EMU. A leak to the pro-EMU newspaper, *The Financial Times* that the government might favour early entry, caused share prices to rise and the pound to fall. Coming at a time when many people felt the pound was overvalued and that this was damaging British industry, this fall in the exchange rate was welcome to many. Indeed some suspected that this was the real purpose of the leak. Subsequently, Gordon Brown gave an interview to *The Times*, a more sceptical organ, in which he appeared to take a more negative stance on early entry. However comments by Gordon Brown's spin doctor Charlie Whelan that Brown was ruling out entry in this Parliament, caused a public relations crisis as the City, the media and the Tories demanded to know what exactly the government's position was.

Gordon Brown announced to the Commons on its return in October 1997 that Labour approved of EMU and would join if it was a success at the first practical moment, which was likely to be early in the next Parliament. He ruled out earlier entry on the grounds that the Conservative government had not prepared the people or the business world for the practical steps necessary. For example, a higher proportion of the British population are homeowners and have their mortgages in the form of variable interest rates, than on the Continent, where renting property is more common, and the norm is a fixed rate loan. British conditions mean that people are particularly sensitive to interest rate changes.

More importantly, the British economy was out of sync with the rest of Europe's. The British economy was in the fifth consecutive year of growth, while the major European economies were only just emerging from recession. It may well be that British conditions will require a more restrictive monetary policy in the form of higher interest rates, just at the time when the opposite is true elsewhere.

The rejection of early entry was disappointing to the TUC, the Liberal Democrats and Britain's European partners but was enough to placate, however temporarily, both wings of the Labour Party. The pro-Europeans took heart from the positive stance on EMU after years of equivocation, and the unambiguous statement that Labour believed it was a purely economic calculation with no constitutional implications. Labour's sceptics were comforted by the thought that Britain was still not committed to join something they believed would go wrong. In their eyes the deflationary stance necessary to create EMU was the very opposite of what Labour should be about – bringing down unemployment and pursuing a more redistributive economic and social policy. If EMU collapsed and Labour had taken Britain in, the fall-out would dwarf that from the ERM fiasco of 1992, and would hand the Conservatives the next election on a plate.

The fear haunting everyone, both government and opposition was that the mistakes over ERM might be repeated but on a greater scale. Gordon Brown was determined that he would not be constrained by question marks over British entry into EMU in the way that Tory Chancellors had been over ERM prior to British entry, when the markets and the media were constantly on the look out for signs that the pound was about to enter. On the other hand the possible gains from British membership of a successful EMU (the creation of an inflation-free zone of currency stability across western Europe) were so tempting that the government did not wish to rule out entry. It could be that inward investment would be hit by any postponement of British entry.

GLOBALISATION

It is always impossible to prove a negative: we cannot know what would have happened to the UK economy since 1973, had it remained outside the European Community. Sceptics argue that because British trade *surplus* with the rest of the world has grown since 1973, while trade *deficit* with the members of the Union has increased, this proves that our economy has suffered and we would have been better off out of the straitjacket of membership. This is dubious logic, just as it is to say that had the UK joined at the outset in 1957 we would have somehow been guaranteed a 'British economic miracle'. What we do know is that business is increasingly international, part of a phenomenon known as **globalisation**. In this way it makes less and less sense to talk of national economies.

The General Agreement on Tariffs and Trade (GATT) was created in 1948 in an attempt to promote the liberalisation of trade. It could be argued that its success in promoting free trade and bringing down barriers to it has rendered institutions such as the EU less necessary. When the EC was set up in the 1950s, there were still numerous barriers to trade; by the 1990s, free trade was 'on the march'; at the end of the Tokyo Round of 1973/79, tariffs for manufactured goods averaged just 5%. At that point GATT was superseded by the World Trade Organisation.

The result of moves towards more and more open economies is that no country is any longer immune from developments elsewhere. Supporters of British membership of EMU such as Ken Clarke argue that if the UK did not join EMU, then British interest rates would have to be higher to persuade the markets that the government was not going to let borrowing rise above the levels permitted by the Maastricht criteria and competitively devalue the pound. Long term British interest rates in 1997 were 1.5 per cent higher than in France or Germany because those countries looked more likely to join EMU.

SUMMARY

The impact of Europe on the British economy is an extremely complex issue, and one which has been subject to much political sloganising. It is certainly true that in the past 25 years the British economy has become more and more integrated with Europe, so that more and more of our trade is with Europe; the crucial exchange rate is that of the pound with the German Mark rather than the pound with the dollar. Whether all of this has been beneficial or detrimental to the British economy remains debatable. It could be argued that the reorientation of Britain's trade, away from her Commonwealth towards Europe, would have happened with or without British entry into the Community, and that the increased interdependence of the global economy means that it is fanciful to believe that the British economy can be in any sense autonomous from Europe.

STUDY GUIDES

This chapter covers a lot of ground! But, the main debates concerning British membership of the European Union have concentrated on the economic aspect, and the tensions within the Conservative Party have tended to focus on questions of political economy, such as should the UK join the Exchange Rate Mechanism?

Your notes need to reflect the importance of the debate about the economic impact on the UK. They need not go into detail about the technical aspects (for example, you do not need to know the economic arguments for and against fixed exchange rates as opposed to floating exchange rates), but you must be clear on how arguments about these issues affected the British political system from 1973 onwards.

It is useful to separate the issues into the following concerns:

• the desire to create a single market
• the debate over the ERM
• the debate over EMU.

You should be aware of the 'line up' of forces over each issue, so that you know who within the British political system supported the creation of the single market, and whether those same people and forces wanted to take it further by creating a single currency. Think about the paradox that the same sceptics who opposed British membership of the ERM and EMU on the grounds that they reduce sovereignty, were quite happy to concede sovereignty over issues such as ownership of British industry.

Consider the following questions:

1   'Events made a monkey out of us'. Discuss the validity of John Major's claim about British Membership of the ERM.

2   Is it correct to say that the issue of Economic and Monetary Union should be decided entirely on its economic merits as it has no constitutional implications?

Both questions require you to revisit one of the most important issues in the relationship between the UK and the European Union – the role of the pound sterling. Both require you to debate certain propositions. In the first case, John Major is claiming that events outside the control of his government conspired to make his policy of entering and remaining within the ERM look foolish.

He presumably had in mind the implications of German reunification, the formal announcement of which coincided in October 1990 with British entry into ERM, and the negative referendum result in Denmark in Summer 1992 which almost derailed the Maastricht Treaty and gave new hope to the Eurosceptics.

You need as well to consider the counter-arguments:

- the rate at which the pound entered ERM was too high and a political mistake
- the decision not to revalue within ERM was wrong
- the attempt to lay the blame on German policy was scapegoating and only served to damage relations with the Union's most important state.

The second essay also provokes a debate. It may well be a good idea to plan it out as a 'yes it is true EMU has no constitutional implications' versus 'no it is not true, EMU has serious implications for the constitution'. Perhaps two columns listing the arguments on both sides would help to structure the essay.

Introduction
define the key terms and indicate the debate

No constitutional implications	**Constitutional Implications**
Two paragraphs looking at the arguments that EMU is essentially an economic not a constitutional issue	Two paragraphs arguing that the issue cuts to the heart of sovereignty/the constitution

Conclusion
It all depends what we mean by constitutional implications, this is ultimately a political dispute, not a factual one

Practice Questions

1   Has membership of the European Union benefited or damaged the UK's economy?
2   'EMU is the most important step towards European integration since the Treaty of Rome'. Discuss.

4

THE IMPACT OF EUROPE ON THE BRITISH CONSTITUTION

Introduction

THIS CHAPTER WILL look at the impact which Europe has had on the British constitution. Since the UK joined the EC in 1973, the rights and wrongs, advantages and disadvantages of British membership have had a major impact on the very constitution.

The United Kingdom is unusual in not having a codified constitution. Its constitution has evolved over the centuries and is to be found in several sources: statute law, common law, conventions, works of authority such as those by Walter Bagehot, editor of *The Economist* in the 1860s, and the great Victorian constitutional theorist, A.V. Dicey, important historical documents such as Magna Carta, as well as European Union law. In general there has been little debate in Britain about constitutional arrangements; many commentators on British politics feel that the British constitution simply 'happened', and the constitution adapts like a living organism, with *flexibility* its main source of strength. Membership of the European Union raises profoundly important constitutional issues particularly concerning the sovereignty of Parliament, the very linchpin of the British constitution since the Glorious Revolution of 1688 created a constitutional monarchy.

One of the most important ways in which membership of the EU has affected the British Constitution and undermined the sovereignty of Parliament, is the fact that it led to the first (and so far, the only) national referendum held in June 1975 on the issue of whether the UK should remain a member. It has led to the suspension of the core constitutional convention of collective responsibility, the overruling of an Act of Parliament and a debate about the Europeanisation of the British constitution.

Key Points

This chapter contains material on the following key issues:

- The impact of membership of the EU on British sovereignty.
- The use of referendums as a way of resolving differences over Europe.
- The European Declaration of Human Rights.
- The third pillar of the Maastricht Treaty, home affairs and justice, which have remained intergovernmental.

SOVEREIGNTY, IN THEORY AND PRACTICE

THE THEORY

Writing at the turn of the century, A.V. Dicey stated that the twin pillars of the British constitution were the rule of law and the sovereignty of Parliament. In 1966, Hinsley defined sovereignty as 'the idea that there is a final and absolute authority in the political community'. A sovereign Parliament is able to pass legislation without fear of being overridden by any other body, such as a Supreme Court. In the USA, laws passed by the Congress and approved by the President can be invalidated by the Federal Supreme Court if it feels that they contravene the constitution.

No such constraint has existed in the UK. The implications were that there were no *legal* limits to the power of Parliament, and no Parliament could bind its successor or be bound by its predecessor. Parliament could make or unmake any laws it wished. Of course there were always *political* limits to its power – it was useless if the UK Parliament were to pass a law banning drinking in Spain, because the law would obviously not be enforced. Yet the absolute supremacy of the British Parliament was felt to be crucial to the notion of the sovereignty of the British state.

Even when on occasions Parliament had devolved power downwards, it could always claim it back:

1 Parliament set up an Assembly for Northern Ireland in 1920, based at Stormont, which was a form of devolution. Yet in 1972 Parliament abolished Stormont, and instituted direct rule over Ulster.
2 In 1963, Parliament created the Greater London Council, but abolished it in 1986.
3 Under the Conservative government from 1979, control over local authority revenue was brought back to central government in Westminster. Firstly the

domestic rate was abolished and replaced with a poll tax, which was then replaced with a council tax. Secondly, the locally determined business rate gave way to the centrally controlled unified business rate. Observers from federalist systems such as Germany, Australia, Canada or the USA must have been amazed by this assertion of central power, yet in a unitary state, subordinate authorities have no guaranteed rights.

NEGATIVE ATTITUDES TO EC MEMBERSHIP

Concerns have always been voiced on the fear of loss of sovereignty which membership of the EC would imply:

- When in July 1961 the Conservative government applied for British membership of the EC, the Conservative rightwinger Derek Walker Smith argued that parliamentary sovereignty was *incompatible* with the acceptance of a treaty that allowed for the supremacy of community law over parliamentary statute.
- The Labour leader Hugh Gaitskell opposed entry on the grounds that it would 'end a thousand years of British history' and represent a betrayal of the Commonwealth.
- The rightwing and fiercely anti-European Conservative MP Enoch Powell argued that sovereignty by its very nature is something that cannot be shared; therefore, by entering the Community, the UK was surrendering its independence. In this sense, the loss of power represented by the British humiliation at Suez in 1956 was not a loss of sovereignty as such, whereas entry into the Community was a surrender of sovereignty because for the first time an external body could overrule Parliament.

SOVEREIGNTY IN PRACTICE

Many commentators, such as the journalists Andrew Marr and Will Hutton, the academics David Judge and Michael Foley, and the politicians Tony Benn and John Biffen, believe that in practice political sovereignty has long rested with the executive – ie, the government. In 1976, the Conservative Lord Hailsham referred to 'elective dictatorship' in the UK. He meant by this that the sovereignty of Parliament had in reality degenerated into the sovereignty of a government, elected by less than half the votes but with a majority of seats in the House of Commons. The government is able to push its legislation through on the grounds that it has a mandate, knowing that the House of Lords have very limited powers to resist and hesitate to use even those for fear of appearing to thwart the will of the elected House.

As David Judge in his book, *The Parliamentary State* puts it,

'EC membership has revealed the contradiction at the heart of the British Constitution; of the principle of parliamentary sovereignty being used by executives to minimise their accountability'.

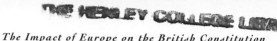

This was very clearly seen in the passage of the Maastricht Treaty through Parliament in 1993. The Tory Whips resorted to an apparently unprecedented degree of pressure, and having lost a major vote on the Treaty, the government demanded that it be tied to a vote of confidence. Tony Benn argued that the government had reversed the decision 'by improper pressure deriving from an undemocratic constitution'.

It could be argued that sovereignty is an outdated concept anyway in the age of the aeroplane, globally mobile capital and increasingly mobile populations. The pro-Europe leftwing publication, *The New Statesman*, argued in June 1990 that sovereignty had already been conceded to international business and that,

---

'to enter into collective social and economic arrangements with other governments is to retrieve sovereignty from the market, not to surrender it to other nations.'

Many British leftwingers traditionally saw Europe as a barrier to socialism, but the British Marxist Tom Nairn has argued that such hostility was based on nationalism not socialism. In his view what concerned socialist MPs such as Michael Foot was really sentimental notions about a defence of parliamentary sovereignty, the British democratic system and Britain as a global power.

Example of sovereignty in practice

In 1976, the Labour government under James Callaghan believed that it faced a growing problem of debt; the public sector borrowing requirement seemed set to rocket. Therefore the government needed a loan from the International Monetary Fund (IMF). The IMF were happy to give such a loan, the biggest in the history of the organisation up to that point, but only on condition that the Labour government abandoned the policies on which it had won office in 1974, and implement monetarist policies. This meant

- reducing public spending, particularly over welfare
- allowing unemployment to rise
- publishing monetary targets.

The Cabinet had lengthy discussions over the terms and although some such as Tony Benn wished to reject them, they were ultimately accepted and no Minister resigned. The Tory Opposition under Margaret Thatcher did not query the right of the IMF to make such policy prescriptions, and in fact it urged the government to accept them. Arguably this acceptance of terms involved a far greater loss of sovereignty than that entailed in joining the ERM or even EMU.

THE FACTORTAME CASE

One of the most eminent British judges of the postwar era Lord Denning warned that the laws of the Community would be like an incoming tide which would wash away much of the traditional common law of Britain. What had been a *potential* power ever since the UK joined the Community, became reality when, with the Factortame case in June 1990, the Merchant Shipping Act of 1988, which banned Spanish fishermen from 'quota hopping', was ruled invalid by the European Court of Justice. In the words of *The New Statesman* in June 1990,

'this is a historic judgement ... it overturns the English ruling that no injunction can be granted against the Crown ... the Europeans are rewriting our constitution.'

At the time of the Factortame judgement the senior judge Lord Bridges pointed out that it was a reaffirmation of the supremacy of Community law, nothing new. However between the UK entering the Community in 1973 and the passage of the Single European Act in 1986, individual states could veto any new proposal. Philip Norton points out that because of Qualified Majority Voting, heavily expanded by the SEA, the British constitution *can* now be changed by directives from Brussels, even though the British may have voted against them. In the debate on the Maastrict Treaty in July 1993 Lady Thatcher specifically referred to the Factortame case as evidence that 'European law will prevail more and more'. She claimed that the Treaty added 111 new policy areas to those covered by QMV, and that this was undesirable.

A Hansard Society Report of January 1993 concluded that,

'not only has the sovereignty of the UK been submerged within a greater entity – the EU – but the delicate balance of power between MPs and the executive is being significantly tilted in favour of the latter by virtue of its role as a tool of Brussels'.

Parliament has generally proved unable to offer effective scrutiny of the EU. Debates over Europe on the floor of the Commons tend to be poorly attended, while the Select Committee on European Legislation has limited powers to look at EU documents and decide whether to recommend debate in the House or examination by a Select Committee. The Lords Select Committee on the European Union has a better reputation, but generates little media interest.

Christopher Booker, a rightwing journalist who has specialised in attacking waste in the Community, argues that Whitehall officials have used British membership as a way of increasing their own power; this is not dissimilar to the view of leftwinger Tony Benn who sees Brussels as a sort of bureaucrat's paradise.

CHANGES IN THE JUDICIARY

Philip Norton argues that although there has been a shift in power from the UK to the institutions of the EU, this has been accompanied by a 'shift of power within the institutions of the UK, with some power shifting to the courts'. During the passage of the Maastricht Treaty, which some opponents wished to have declared unlawful by the courts, the Speaker of the Commons had to remind the judges of the legislative supremacy of Parliament established in 1689.

British judges were traditionally said to be 'more executive-minded than the executive' and therefore very reluctant to challenge the government. This began to change by the 1970s, as the judges declared certain actions of the then Labour government to be beyond its powers (*ultra vires*). At the time, commentators such as Professor Griffith put this down to an inherently conservative judiciary seeking to block socialism. However, through the 1980s and 1990s, an even more activist judiciary overruled Conservative governments on a regular basis.

Partly, this was a product of a new generation of judges increasingly influenced by European jurisprudence where judges are more politically exposed. All the other member states have codified constitutions which are interpreted by some form of Supreme Court. In Germany, the Constitutional Court has to interpret the 1949 German Constitution – for example in 1993, it ruled that the Maastricht Treaty was constitutional. European practices were bound to have some influence on the British judges, even if they are working within a different constitutional, political and legal context. In recent years the British government has had to bring in changes to pensions, social security and equal opportunities in order to bring British law into line with European law.

THE 1975 REFERENDUM

By 1998, referendums have become an accepted feature of the British constitution, with referenda on devolution for Scotland and Wales, one for London on the idea of a directly elected Mayor, a promised referendum on EMU, and on changing the electoral system. However, before 1973, there had never been a major referendum within the UK.

In 1969 a Tory backbencher, Bruce Campbell, called for a referendum on Europe on the grounds that with all three parties in favour, there was no way of expressing opposition at an election. His motion was signed by 55 MPs, but no referendum was held, and during the 1970 election all the party leaders opposed one. However by the end of 1970, the senior Labour politician James Callaghan noted that the idea of a referendum was a 'little rubber life raft into which the whole party may one day have to climb'. Edward Heath led Britain into the EC without a referendum, but a few months later, George Pompidou, President of France 1969–74, called a referendum in France on the principle of enlarging the Community; British Eurosceptics such as Enoch Powell and Tony Benn took up the idea. Referenda followed in Denmark, Ireland and Norway which rejected entry.

The most prominent anti-European Tory Enoch Powell left the party in 1974, and advised people to vote Labour on the grounds that they might well take the UK out of the Community. Powell's biographer, Patrick Cosgrove, claims that his intervention was crucial in the very close elections of 1974. Labour was the biggest party following the February 1974 election, and formed a minority government even though the Tories won more votes. At the election of October 1974, Labour won an overall majority of just three, subsequently eroded by by-election defeats.

PRESSURE ON THE GOVERNMENT

Labour's pro-European Deputy Leader Roy Jenkins resigned in 1972 when the party leader, Harold Wilson, in order to keep the left of the party from outright opposition, accepted the Bennite demand for a referendum asking the people of the UK whether they wished to remain within the EC. Referendums had been discussed before as way of resolving disagreement, and in 1973 the first ever referendum had been held in the UK, when the people of Northern Ireland were asked whether they wished to stay in the UK. However it is surely no coincendence that it was the thorny issue of Europe which promoted the first *national* referendum.

Conservative Party leader Margaret Thatcher, quoting the former Labour PM Attlee, opposed it as 'it would bind and fetter parliamentary sovereignty'. She argued that there is a system of representative democracy in the UK, so to then introduce referendums, a form of direct democracy, would appear to

- undermine the role of MPs
- impinge on the power of Parliament
- make collective responsibility and party unity more difficult to maintain.

Yet, Wilson saw a referendum as a way of keeping his divided party together. With sixteen Cabinet Ministers in favour and seven against, Wilson suspended collective responsibility on the matter and Ministers were allowed to speak their mind *outside* Parliament. This was the first time collective responsibility had been suspended since 1931. When Eric Heffer, a junior Minister in the Department of Industry, opposed membership in a speech in the Commons, Wilson sacked him.

In Bulmer and Roberts's opinion 'the changes negotiated by Labour were more cosmetic than of actual importance but were recommended by the government to the people'. However not all commentators agree Labour had not effected any changes of significance, and neither does the man who negotiated the terms, Callaghan who in his memoirs argues that the renegotiation paved the way for Thatcher in her attempt at getting a better budget deal for Britain.

THE RESULTS

Up until a few weeks before referendum, the opinion polls had showed a majority *against* membership. However, in the referendum, the majority in favour of continued membership was about 2:1 (67.2 per cent) with a turnout of about 64 per cent. This meant that about 43 per cent of those entitled to vote had voted in favour, and only 22 per cent of adults had voted against. Anderton argues that this marked the first real popular participation in the movement towards European unity, not only in the UK but across Europe. This could have resolved the issue for good – the losing side formally accepted defeat – but the issue refused to go away. Eurosceptics such as the former Conservative Party chairman Norman Tebbit, argue that the people were deceived over the full implications of British membership. The Thatcherite academic Martin Holmes argues that the case for membership was presented in almost entirely *economic* terms, rather than as the political issue he felt it should have been, quoting the government's 'Why You Should Vote Yes' leaflet which claimed:

'inside the Market we can get more money spent on Britain … more from the Social Fund for retraining workers … more from Coal and Steel funds and the European Investment Bank'.

Even Edward Heath's biographer, John Campbell, accepts that

'there is a case for saying that Parliament in 1971 and the country in 1975 was hoodwinked into signing up for more than it was ever told … ultimate political union may have been implicit in 1975, but it was certainly not explicit'.

The official government pamphlet of the time stated that 'no important new policy can be decided in Brussels or anywhere else without the consent of a British Minister answerable to a British government and British parliament'. The Eurosceptic Referendum Party was to repeat these words in the 1997 British General Election campaign, arguing that the public had been consistently misled over Europe.

THE RETURN OF REFERENDUMS

There were referendums in 1979 on devolution for Scotland and Wales, but no more national referendums. In the debate before the Maastricht Treaty in late 1991, Tony Benn and Margaret Thatcher demanded a referendum on a single currency. Thatcher argued that with the leadership of all three main parties in favour of a single currency, voters would have no opportunity to show their views. Edward Heath reminded Thatcher of her former opposition to referendums – 'I agree with her (earlier view) entirely.' Thatcher responded that, in June 1975 she was simply being loyal to the policy she had inherited as leader in February of that year, but that her own personal wish had been to 'let the people speak'. As Prime Minister, John Major commented, 'We are a parliamentary democracy and I can see no need for a referendum'.

A BLOW TO THE MAASTRICHT TREATY?

John Major signed the Maastricht Treaty in December 1991, and was able to take a relatively united Conservative Party into the election of April 1992 and pull off a surprise victory. However in June 1992, the political landscape changed when Denmark rejected the Treaty in a referendum by 5 per cent. Major responded by claiming that, at Maastricht, Europe had moved away from centralised power, but the British Eurosceptics applauded the Danes. Ninety MPs (including Ulster Unionists) signed an Early Day Motion calling for a 'fresh start' on Europe, and demanded that the British people be allowed their say. The ratification of the Maastricht bill brought demands for a referendum; these demands were strengthened by the ERM crisis of September 1992 which, the sceptics argued, proved the folly of EMU.

The decisive endorsement of Maastricht by the Irish referendum in June (69.1 per cent) was overshadowed by the narrowness of the French result on September 20th, when only 51.04 per cent voted for it. The majority of the French political elite, led by President Mitterand and Valerie Giscard D'Estaing (President of France 1974–1981) argued that Maastricht would restrict German power, but opponents such as Segun argued that monetary union would lead to German hegemony. It could well be that the large hostile vote was simply a reflection of the unpopularity of Mitterand by 1992, rather than the unpopularity of the Treaty on European Union. Opponents of referenda such as Roy Hattersley argue that this is what happens in such cases: people use the referendum as a protest vote so that you do not get an accurate reflection of opinion on the issue at stake. Regardless of this, the closeness of the French result gave further encouragement to the British sceptics.

The Thatcherite slogan was 'a blow against the Maastricht Treaty is a blow for people's power'. Critics pointed out the irony that the Thatcher years had been the clearest example of elective dictatorship, with the government pushing through Parliament legislation such as the poll tax and the abolition of the Greater London Council, without serious concern for the 'rights' of Parliament or the objections of significant numbers of people. Yet now, the same politicians were demanding that the people be given a direct say, because Parliament was inadequate for the task of representing the people's will.

In April 1993, the Commons rejected a referendum on the Maastricht Treaty by 124 to 363, with Labour rebels such as Tony Benn, Bryan Gould and Frank Field voting alongside Tories such as Rhodes Boyson in voting for a referendum. In May 1993, a second referendum in Denmark had approved the Treaty by 56.8 per cent, but in the year between the two Danish referendums, support Europe-wide for the Maastricht Treaty had plummeted, five currencies had been devalued, and two of those (the pound and the lira) were outside the ERM.

During the debate in the Lords in July 1993, Lady Thatcher argued that,

'We have surrendered too many powers already. We should surrender no more unless the people wish it. It is the people's turn to speak'.

The referendum proposal was defeated on a three line whip by 445 to 176.

THE REFERENDUM PARTY

By the late 1990s the Tory sceptic and former Chancellor, Norman Lamont, was still claiming that 'Britain's membership of the EU has not been settled for all time; it is provisional, not unconditional'. Lamont, other senior Tories and businessmen who backed the Tory Party such as Paul Sykes, demanded a referendum on at least EMU if not indeed on the broader issue of membership of the EU. The billionaire businessman Sir James Goldsmith formed the Referendum Party to promote the idea of referendum on Europe in general and EMU in particular. He was supported by the former Tory Party Treasurer and close ally of Margaret Thatcher, Lord McAlpine, Thatcher's former Economics Adviser Sir Alan Walters, and later by the Eurosceptic MP George Gardiner. Goldsmith prepared to spend over £20 million financing the party. One leaked document warned that the Referendum Party could cost the Tories 25 seats in a general election.

It was in response to such fears that, in spring 1996, John Major conceded a referendum on EMU. However, even then it had to be couched in such a way as to keep the pro-Europeans Kenneth Clarke and Michael Heseltine content; indeed, on March 13th, Clarke had to downplay talk of his resignation. A referendum would only be held when the Conservative government had decided that the conditions for British entry into EMU were right, and Parliament had voted for it. Under such circumstances, collective responsibility would be upheld so that opponents of EMU would have to resign if they wished to campaign for a 'no' vote. The Labour leadership, both in opposition and government, made it clear that once the Cabinet had taken a decision, then it would be binding on the whole government through collective responsibility. Tony Blair was not going to repeat the Wilson formula of 1975, probably because to do so would expose divisions within the Labour Party, leading to cross-party coalitions as Labour opponents made common cause with Conservative opponents.

CONSTITUTIONAL REFORM

It could be argued that the EU is pushing the British into reforming their constitution. The Labour Party has traditionally favoured a strong central state, hence their support for the first-past-the-post electoral system even for non-governmental bodies such as the European Parliament; they opposed a Bill of Rights right through until the 1990s on the grounds that it would protect individual right such as the right to private education, at the expense of collective rights such as the right to work, and would give more power to judges who (in the view of people such as Tony Benn) were often reactionary so would use that power against Labour governments, and expressed lukewarm support for devolution within the UK. 'Old Labour' was as concerned as many Conservatives to protect the sovereignty of the British state so that in office Labour would have untrammelled power.

Since coming to power in 1997, 'New Labour' has

- devolved power over interest rates to the Bank of England
- appeared willing to consider reform of the voting system
- increased powers for local authorities with directly elected executive mayors
- fully supported devolution for Scotland and to a lesser extent Wales (in both cases the Assemblies to be elected by a form of Proportional Representation, common on the continent)
- embraced a form of PR for the 1999 European elections
- been prepared to put the European Declaration of Human Rights into British law.

They have argued for a more pluralist political system in which power is spread around. In such a context, their willingness to concede a degree of power to Europe was consistent.

However, Labour has never accepted the case for a federal Europe. As EC President, Jacques Delors denied that federalism meant the creation of a superstate; on the contrary, it meant a decentralised political system. Labour and Conservatives have distanced themselves from this notion, yet at the same time Labour is offering federal-style solutions domestically with devolution for Scotland and Wales and a sharing of power over Northern Ireland. Under devolution, the Westminster Parliament remains sovereign but concedes a degree of autonomy to Scotland and Wales. Over Ulster, the UK government is willing to concede power-sharing, involving the Dublin government. In some ways the logical conclusion of this process could be said to be a federal United Kingdom in a federal Europe. The Liberal Democrats are willing to accept the argument in its entirety, but so far they are unique in so doing.

Liberal Democrats are the true believers in **subsidiarity**, the principle whereby decisions should be reached at the lowest tier of government compatible with efficiency. In this approach, the nation state is regarded as too small a body to make effective decisions over, for example, acid rain, and too large and remote a body to make democratic decisions over, for example, educational provision. Some decisions have to be taken by the nation state, and others have to be taken by bodies above the state, but many decisions can be taken by regional or local bodies. This line of thinking leads more to a Europe of the regions than to the centralised federal superstate of sceptic nightmares.

Stephen George argues that the adversarial nature of the British political system separates most British politicians from their European counterparts. All the other member states have codified constitutions, many have federal arrangements, and all use some form of proportional representation. These encourage a more decentralised, consensual political order, which is what the British Liberal Democrats favour. Now that Labour is working with the Liberals over constitutional reform, this may be the direction in which the country will move. This appears to be the implication of the decision to incorporate the European Declaration of Human Rights into domestic law.

THE EUROPEAN DECLARATION OF HUMAN RIGHTS

The British government was the first to sign the European Declaration of Human Rights in 1950. The Declaration is enforced by the European Court of Human Rights, which is often confused with the European Court of Justice. However unlike the ECJ, the European Court of Human Rights has, so far, no power of enforcement in the United Kingdom.

The rights protected by the Declaration are civil and political, and include:

* Articles 2 and 5 – the right to life, liberty and security of the person
* Article 3 – the prohibition of torture, inhuman or degrading treatment
* Article 6 – the right to a fair trial and access to justice in criminal and civil matters
* Article 8 – respect for private and family life, home and correspondence
* Article 9 – the right to freedom of thought, conscience and religion
* Article 10 – free expression, including freedom of the press
* Article 11 – freedom of assembly and association, including the right to join a trade union.

Since 1966, British citizens have enjoyed under Article 25 the right to petition the European Court of Human Rights in Strasbourg. Although the process is lengthy and expensive, many people have availed themselves of this right. The result has been that the British government has lost more cases there than any other signatory. Unlike every other member state except Ireland, the British government has always refused to incorporate the convention into domestic law, without which the rulings of the Commission are not binding on British courts.

Yet when the Commission has ruled against the British government over a range of cases, from prisoners' rights to homosexuals in the Armed Forces, to caning in schools, to newspaper coverage of the treatment of thalidomide victims in the 1960s, the British government has almost always complied with the rulings. The exceptions have been over terrorism in Northern Ireland. When in 1988 the ECHR ruled that elements of the Prevention of Terrorism Act were contrary to the Declaration, the Thatcher government refused to alter the law, arguing that the situation was extreme and required strict laws to combat the IRA.

Even in the absence of incorporation into domestic law, the Convention has had a big impact. No government likes to be embarrassed by declarations that it has contravened rights and there have been arrangements for 'Strasbourg-proofing' legislation to make sure that it complies with the Convention. The Convention is cited in British courts; in July 1996 Lord Chief Justice Bingham stated that courts do try to conform to the Convention. Even so, cases took five years to reach Strasbourg and Ministers such as the then Home Secretary Michael Howard made it plain that they did not regard the ECHR as a serious constraint. This is why campaigners wanted its enforcement in British courts.

In April 1996 at the height of the BSE row, the Tory sceptic Ian Duncan-Smith introduced a bill to curb the powers of the European Court of Justice; 66 Tories backed him. By then the Tory Cabinet was actually debating whether the UK should withdraw from the European Convention on Human Rights. Duncan-Smith survived the May 1997 election, and is currently a key figure within William Hague's Shadow Cabinet.

At the 1992 General Election, Labour was against incorporation of the ECHR into domestic law. This reflected 'Old Labour's' hostility towards potentially reactionary judges. Things have changed, since the 1997 General Election, and with the backing of the Lord Chancellor Lord Irvine, and other senior figures such as the Foreign Secretary Robin Cook and the Chancellor, Gordon Brown, the Labour government under Tony Blair is now going to give the Declaration statutory force in the UK, so that it will act as a surrogate Bill of Rights.

The Home Secretary Jack Straw described this process as 'bringing rights home' and the move was warmly welcomed by the various civil liberties pressure groups, although they differed over the precise mechanisms required to ensure that rights were safeguarded. As it stands, the courts will *not* be able to strike down an Act of Parliament as contrary to the Convention; they will merely be able to draw attention to the breach of rights. This is known as a 'soft' form of incorporation similar to that found in New Zealand. What campaigners had favoured was 'hard' incorporation, so that the judges would be able to overrule legislation if it contravened rights (as the judges can do in Canada). Similarly, campaigners had wanted the appointment of a Rights Commission to oversee the workings of the act.

HOME AFFAIRS AND JUSTICE

Few issues raise such sensitive concerns for a sovereign state as immigration, border control and inter-state policing. It is no coincidence that the occasions when the British government flouted the rulings of the ECHR were over its rulings on the Prevention of Terrorism Act. As far back as 1975, the then British Home Secretary James Callaghan suggested cooperation against organised crime and terrorism. This led to the TREVI Group (terrorism/radicalism/extremism/violence/international) which aimed to reduce international crime and in particular terrorist activity. Of course, the British and Irish governments have particular reason to fear terrorism given that the IRA campaign is the bloodiest terror campaign in Europe, having claimed the lives of over 3,000 people since 1968. It makes the two governments understandably rather sensitive to issues of border control.

By 1985 France, Germany and the Benelux states signed an agreement at **Schengen** to eliminate border controls between their countries. Italy joined them in 1990, with Spain and Portugal joining in 1991. At the time of the Maastricht Treaty, federalists wanted the European Court of Justice to have a supranational role to play in the third pillar of the treaty, home affairs and justice. Germany was particularly keen that the Commission should have a role regarding the cross-border aspects of the crime. The Tories opposed this throughout the 1980s and 1990s, arguing for a purely intergovernmental approach building on TREVI. Europol, a form of coordination of European police efforts, was created to cover drug dealing, terrorism and international crime.

Demands for further integration over home affairs and justice resurfaced in the 1996/97 Inter Governmental Conference. The Conservative Government of Britain alone wanted to reduce the power of the European Court of Justice. They refused to consider even a limited use of majority voting in foreign and security policy, immigration or cross-border cooperation on policing and justice. The Home Secretary Michael Howard blocked the other 14 states from making the embryonic European police force, Europol, subject to the ECJ. Labour's Shadow Home Secretary, Jack Straw appeared to support this intergovernmentalist line on the third pillar. Labour felt they simply could not afford to be seen to be 'soft' on such issues.

In February 1995, a junior Minister at the Home Office, Charles Wardle, resigned over fear of an 'unchecked flow of vast numbers of people incurring a huge cost on social security, health, education etc.'. His fear was the Schengen Agreement to remove border controls among participating states, which came into force on March 26th 1995, ten years after the original agreement in the Luxembourg village of Schengen. However, in practice, France still imposes frontier restrictions because of alleged drug-running from Holland. To the dismay of people such as Pauline Green, leader of Labour's MEPs, Labour even appeared to support Wardle's warnings on immigration. Green, EC Commissioner Neil Kinnock and Labour MEP Glenys Kinnock dismissed the warnings of mass immigration into the UK if frontier controls were abolished, as 'a complete travesty'.

Labour had fought the 1994 European elections on the right of free movement within the EU for EU citizens and legal immigrants, but in a speech in 1995 Jack Straw insisted,

'our position has always been that the issue of border controls and immigration policy must be for the UK government to determine and not for the European institutions,'

and tried to silence Labour MEPs on the issue. There are clear limits to the Euro-enthusiasm of even New Labour, and those limits are clearly reached on this issue.

SUMMARY

Despite the disappointment felt in some quarters over the manner of incorporation of the European Declaration of Human Rights into British domestic law, it is clear that the move will have major implications for the British legal and political systems. Nor is it the only important change in the offing. By the end of 1997, the Prime Minister Tony Blair had set up a commission to consider electoral reform under the Chairmanship of the Liberal Democrat, Lord Jenkins. It is possible that the UK will continue with its first-past-the-post electoral system for the elections to the House of Commons, and that the 'Europeanisation' of the British constitution will turn out to be rather limited, especially if the Conservatives make an early return to power. However, the more likely scenario is that the British constitution will become more and more affected by 'Europe', just as Britain's political parties have already been.

It is useful to consider issues of sovereignty as shown in table 3:

Table 3: *Changes to British Sovereignty*		
LEGAL SOVEREIGNTY	POLITICAL SOVEREIGNTY	ECONOMIC SOVEREIGNTY
Pre-1973: resided with Parliament	Throughout the twentieth century, has resided in the Executive	With globalisation, the concept becomes irrelevant
Passage of the 1972 European Communities Act changes everything	Entry into the EEC gives more power to the Executive	The SEA speeds up the process and leads inevitably to demands for EMU
EMU continues a process begun in 1972	Joining EMU takes power *away* from the British Executive	EMU will affect the UK whether it joins or not

STUDY GUIDES

Revision Hints

This chapter takes us to the heart of the debates about the impact that membership of the European Union has had on the previously rather insular British political system. Your notes need to be clear as to the nature of that constitution prior to British entry, and the changes brought about by it. In particular you must look at the key concept of sovereignty, both legal and political. Be aware of the debates on whether British membership of what is now the European Union involved a loss of sovereignty, and if so, how this is manifested, or whether in reality, Parliament had long since ceased to be sovereign because the Executive was dominant.

You also need to be clear as to the differing political positions on sovereignty, so that the leftwing view that sovereignty has already been conceded to international capital is distinct from the rightwing view that sovereignty is indivisible.

Your notes should also cross-refer back to the historical account in chapters 2 and 3, and look at the way in which early concerns about sovereignty have reappeared in recent years. Similarly, you should refer back to chapter 3 on the economic impact, and in particular the section on the Single European Act, to consider whether in practice this involved a loss of sovereignty greater than that conceded previously or since.

1   Had Parliament ceased to be sovereign before the UK entered the European Community?

2   'Europe is rewriting our constitution for us.' Discuss.

It is vital that you understand that politics is a *social* science, in which there are differing theoretical approaches and relatively few hard facts. The concept of sovereignty illustrates this point particularly well. Even though it is one of the most important concepts in the whole of political philosophy, there is no agreement on precisely what is meant by it. You have already seen that the same is true of other crucial concepts such as subsidiarity and federalism. For the first essay you need to consider the differing meanings of sovereignty, legal and political, and you need to look at the argument that Parliament had long since conceded power to the Executive, to big business and to international institutions such as NATO and the International Monetary Fund.

The second essay requires you to consider ways in which membership of the European Union and contact with other European institutions such as the ECHR is driving forward constitutional change. It needs consideration of the ability of the European Court of Justice to overrule Parliament, but also of the more subtle influence of the ECHR as well as the pressures towards introducing PR for European elections. It is necessary to discuss the ways in which the concept of subsidiarity, popularised by John Major in 1992 as a way of preserving certain powers from the reach of the EU, has the potential to backfire by raising demand for genuine subsidiarity, that is the maximum devolution of power downwards. This can be linked with the new constitutional reform agenda on which the Labour government is working with the Liberal Democrats, to recast the British state in a way which reflects European arrangements – an independent central bank, devolution, PR for more and more institutions.

1   'Membership of the European Union has affected the essential elements of the British Constitution.' Discuss.
2   To what extent has membership of the European Union taken power away from British politicians?

5

THE IMPACT OF EUROPE ON THE BRITISH POLITICAL PARTIES

Introduction

THIS CHAPTER WILL consider the impact of the European issue upon Britain's main political parties. In democracies all great parties are inevitably coalitions of different groups who come together under the umbrella of a party and attempt to minimise their differences in order to maintain a notion of party cohesion. This is particularly true with countries that have a first-past-the-post form of electoral system. Presenting a united front is always more crucial for the governing party because voters punish division, hence the importance of collective responsibility, one of the key conventions of the British constitution. Disagreement and dissent are vital and within certain limits a sign of a healthy, mature party. However, if the disagreement gets too far out of hand, then it can help to weaken the party. This is arguably what happened to Labour over the European issue in the 1970s and 1980s when it helped split the party, and could be said to be happening to the Tories in the 1990s when the issue may yet split the Conservatives.

Key Points
This chapter contains material on the following key issues:

- The divisions within the Conservative Party.
- The divisions within the Labour Party.
- The attitude of the Liberal Democrats.
- The importance of the European issue in the British General Election of 1997.

THE CONSERVATIVE PARTY

The Economist claimed in November 1994, 'Europe involves questions of nationality, identity and sovereignty that threaten to destroy the Conservative Party'. It could be said to have destroyed both Margaret Thatcher and John Major, and is causing severe difficulties for William Hague. Yet it was the Conservative leader Winston Churchill who in 1946 called for a United States of Europe, a Conservative Prime Minister Harold Macmillan who in 1961 first tried to take the UK into Europe, and another Conservative Prime Minister Edward Heath, who eventually led the country into the EC.

Edward Heath represents the 'One Nation' tradition within the Tory Party, named after the great nineteenth century Tory Prime Minister Benjamin Disraeli who argued that the party must aim to bridge the gulf between the two nations, the poor and the rich, and create 'one nation'. This paternalist approach has always coexisted with the free market ideas of people such as Enoch Powell and Margaret Thatcher. New Right Conservatives are sometimes referred to as neo-liberal because they have adopted the classical liberal idea of *laissez faire*, leading to a minimal state. For most of the twentieth century, paternalist Tories such as Churchill, Macmillan, Anthony Eden and Heath dominated the party. However in the last 20 or so years, the situation has been reversed. It is too much of a simplification to say that 'One Nation' Tories are always pro-European and 'New Right' Conservatives are always sceptic, but generally speaking this is the case. However, by the 1990s, even previously enthusiastic European Tories such as David Hunt MP were sounding less positive about Europe.

THE THATCHER YEARS

The replacement of the Europhile Edward Heath by the much more sceptical Margaret Thatcher as Tory leader in February 1975 was clearly a turning point in the party's relationship with the EU. Thatcher had been a loyal member of the Heath Cabinet which had taken the UK into the Community, but she was much less enthusiastic about anything resembling political union. However, when she became Tory leader in 1975 and Prime Minister in 1979, the party was relatively united over Europe. No Tories had followed Powell out of the party, and although a section remained opposed to British membership, they were not a vocal force. It was Labour which at that stage was seen as anti-Europe, a stance which Thatcher attacked as extremist.

The first ever direct elections to the European Parliament took place in 1979. The decision to introduce direct elections was taken while Labour was in power, and was supposed to:

- make the Community more democratically accountable to the people of Europe
- balance the introduction of the European Council, ie, institutionalised meetings of the heads of government of member states, in the mid-1970s.

Many in the then Labour government had been hostile to direct elections, and in 1979 the turn out in the UK was one of the lowest within the Community – only about one-third of the population bothered to vote.

MARGARET THATCHER ATTENDING A EUROPEAN SUMMIT IN 1984

The first Thatcher term was dominated by disputes over its macroeconomic policies, and in particular its refusal to reverse those when unemployment rocketed. By 1982 with victory in the Falklands War, the Labour Party split and the economy beginning to recover, the government in general and Margaret Thatcher especially recovered in the opinion polls, and went on to win a landslide victory in June 1983. Europe had hardly featured except as 'background noise', with Thatcher demanding a refund on Britain's contributions. This played well as a patriotic tactic and helped reinforce the image of the 'Iron Lady' unafraid of anyone – the Soviets, the Argentineans, the IRA or the Europeans.

In 1984, the Conservatives defeated Labour again in the elections to the European Parliament. According to the former broadcaster John Cole at the European elections of June 1984, Labour's 'lack of interest in Europe caused Labour candidates to be punished by the voters'; the Tories won 45 seats to Labour's 32.

By the mid 1980s, party positions on Europe had started to shift. The Labour Party was becoming more pro-Europe just at the same time that the Conservative government was starting to divide over the issue. The second Thatcher term (1983 to 1987) saw the beginnings of a rift within the party which was to grow ever wider.

THE WESTLAND CRISIS 1986

By January 1986 the then Defence Secretary Michael Heseltine and Trade Secretary Leon Brittan had resigned over the scandal involving the Westland Helicopter Company. At one level the issue was relatively trivial – should Westland be taken over by an American company or by a European Consortium? Margaret Thatcher and Leon Brittan argued that the company should go to the highest bidder, even if this was American. Michael Heseltine argued that for strategic and political reasons, it would be better if Britain's sole surviving helicopter manufacturer was kept in European hands. It was sold to the American company, and Heseltine resigned out of principle. Leon Brittan's resignation that January followed his instructions to a Civil Servant, Collette Bowe, to leak a letter from the Attorney General to Michael Heseltine.

At another level, the crisis was extremely important to the British constitution because it raised issues of collective responsibility, Prime Ministerial power, the role of the Civil Service and of Select Committees of the Commons. Westland was certainly a turning point, because the resignation of two key Ministers was the real beginning of a divide within the highest reaches of the Conservative Party, a divide that was to cost more and more ministerial 'scalps' over the next few years.

THE BRUGES SPEECH 1988

The Westland crisis did not prevent the Tories winning a third term in 1987, and in many ways Margaret Thatcher was in a stronger position at the start of that term than at any other moment.

- Labour was in disarray and having to re-examine its policies.
- The Alliance was breaking up, with the majority of Liberals and the SDP fusing to form the Liberal Democrats but with a rump under SDP Leader David Owen refusing to join.
- Thatcher's main rival within the party (Heseltine) appeared to have self-destructed over Westland.
- The economy was booming.
- Thatcher enjoyed very good relations with the heads of both superpowers, Ronald Reagan and Mikhail Gorbachev.

This was the point at which Thatcherites woke up to the wider political implications of the single market, and in particular to what the New Right saw as the threat posed by the 'social dimension' ideas of President of the EC, Jacques Delors. It was in this context that Thatcher outlined her own views of how Europe should develop.

In September 1988, Thatcher declared in her Bruges speech that the Community should be a free trade zone *without* political ambitions. She had not spent nine years rolling back the frontiers of the state at home, only to see them rolled forward by the federalist bureaucracy of Brussels headed by the French Socialist Jacques Delors. She called for a *Europe des patries* of the sort favoured by De Gaulle. In the words of the academic John Gray in an article in *The Guardian* in 1988, the intergovernmentalist vision is of

> *'a Europe of diverse nation states sharing a common cultural inheritance and having common policies on trade and defence',*

or as the journalist John Palmer puts it, 'a depoliticised common market stretching from the Atlantic to Vladivostock'. She also attacked the Common Agricultural Policy, arguing that it was in need of reform.

THE EUROPEAN ELECTIONS OF 1989

The economic boom of the late 1980s had ended with interest rates rising and the British economy moving towards recession. May 1989 saw the tenth anniversary of Margaret Thatcher coming to power, and Labour Party leader Neil Kinnock declared the elections to the European Parliament in June 1989 as a referendum on 10 years of Thatcherism. In these elections, the Conservatives suffered their first national defeat at the hands of Labour since October 1974. Labour won 45 seats on 40.1 per cent of the votes, to the Tories 32 seats on 34.7 per cent. The turn-out at just 36 per cent was the lowest of any member state. The Tory MEPs blamed the hostility of the Westminster leadership and the negative slogan 'living on a diet of Brussels'; Thatcher blamed the organisers of the campaign including Peter Brooke, the then Chairman. This was the only national election Thatcher ever lost. As John Cole puts it in an article in *The New Statesman*,

> *'it was the poor performance of the Tories, the boost these gave to Labour, that set off a worrying period in by-elections and local government elections. These initiated the Conservative loss of morale that made her party decide she was no longer an election winner.'*

CABINET RESHUFFLES

The rifts within the Tory party were becoming more and more obvious. Just before her departure for the key Madrid summit in June 1989, Margaret Thatcher was told by her Chancellor, Nigel Lawson, and her Foreign Secretary, Geoffrey

unless she stipulated the conditions under which the pound would
ney would resign. Thatcherites such as Nicholas Ridley and Norman
e that no Prime Minister should be subject to such 'ambushes', and
that she should have called their bluff. Instead of this, she *did* publicly state her
conditions for entry, which involved:

- convergence of inflation rates
- progress towards liberalisation of financial services within the single market.

The Madrid meeting was a vital development, because it:

- approved the Delors Report on EMU
- agreed to begin Stage 1 from July 1990 whereby *all* members states should join
  the ERM
- set up an intergovernmental conference to make preparations for EMU.

Thatcher stated that she was unwilling to go beyond Stage 1, and on her return
got her 'revenge' by demoting Howe in a major Cabinet reshuffle (he was
removed from the Foreign Office and made Leader of the Commons). His
replacement was the relatively unknown Chief Secretary to the Treasury, John
Major. Major had only been in the Cabinet for two years, and it was assumed that
Thatcher wanted a more compliant colleague to head a department she had long
distrusted. As compensation, Howe was made Deputy Prime Minister, but it was
clear that this was an honorary title only.

THE DEPARTURE OF THATCHER, NOVEMBER 1990

The list of resignations over Europe was growing – Michael Heseltine, Leon
Brittan, Nigel Lawson and Nicholas Ridley, who resigned in July 1990 over an
interview in *The Spectator* in which he had criticised Germany. The resignations
weakened Thatcher's authority and focused attention on the party's divisions
over Europe; the policy differences became tangled up with the question of her
leadership and the succession to it. Europe had become the battleground for the
future direction of Conservative policy. Unlike Labour's divisions in the 1970s,
Tory divisions were not as clear cut as, should we stay in, or leave? Conservatives
were divided over the future *direction* of the Community.

The list of resignations lengthened on November 1st 1990 when Geoffrey Howe
announced his departure from the government. This followed a European
Council meeting in Rome where Thatcher had been isolated in her opposition to
the setting up of an intergovernmental conference on EMU. In her memoirs,
Thatcher blames Glulio Andreotti, 'even I was unprepared for the way things
went'. Her anger at Andreotti's ambush finished her.

Geoffrey Howe objected to Thatcher's relentless negativism towards Europe, her
habit of saying 'No, no, no'. She had even sabotaged her own Chancellor's option

of a soft ECU. In his resignation speech ten days later, Howe argued that if Britain did not become centrally involved in the debate on EMU, it would be left behind. Howe twisted the knife in the wound, and effectively invited Michael Heseltine to challenge Thatcher for the leadership. The following day Heseltine provoked a leadership contest, but the beneficiary was to be John Major.

Europe was definitely not the *only* issue behind Thatcher's downfall, but it was a powerful contributory factor. Major brought Heseltine back into the Cabinet for the first time since January 1986. Hurd remained Foreign Secretary and Major's campaign manager Norman Lamont was rewarded with the Chancellorship.

JOHN MAJOR AND 'THE HEART OF EUROPE'

John Major was not allowed to be more pro-European because his own party would not let him. His Cabinet still contained a sizeable number of Thatcherites such as Michael Howard and Peter Lilley, and a growing number of Tory MPs were moving towards a more sceptical stance on European integration. As Ian Aitken puts it 'by then the Conservative Party had long since ceased to be the party of Europe, and had become the party of English nationalism'. In Stephen George's words Labour had 'become the more European of the two major parties'. Liberal Democrat leader Paddy Ashdown argued that Major had simply replaced 'no, no, no' with 'maybe, maybe, maybe'.

Intergovernment conferences (IGC) on political, economic and monetary union opened in December 1990. They provided an essential forum for thrashing out amendments to the Treaty of Rome. The last IGC had paved the way for the SEA in 1986, and sceptics worried that this time they might lead to what Margaret Thatcher called a 'conveyor belt to federalism'.

The Gulf War of January to March 1991 distracted attention from European issues. The war was won with very light casualties on the Allied side, and there was talk of Major exploiting the patriotic feeling to call an election in spring 1991. However, with a major European summit coming up at the end of 1991 in Holland, Major delayed the election in the hope that he could unite his party around a moderate European position. Had Major won an early election with a reasonable majority, maybe things would have been very different.

THE TREATY OF MAASTRICHT DECEMBER 1991

In June 1991, at the same moment that the Yugoslav Federation was beginning to fall apart, the Commission published its draft treaty which had provision for a single currency, a central bank, a common foreign and security policy as well as common industrial, social, employment, environment, health and education policies. This was therefore 'federal' in its scope. Jacques Delors always argued that federalism meant a dispersal of power rather than its concentration. He claimed that federalism actually implies a *decentralised* political system where some functions are delegated to a higher authority in return for specific benefits. Both major British parties rejected this interpretation and still do, seeing federalism as involving a concentration of power in Brussels. The Conservatives also rejected the Delors plan for EMU which Labour accepted in principle.

During the autumn of 1991 the debate over Europe became once more vitriolic. The Dutch had offered the British an opt-out on EMU, but sceptics thought this inadequate. In December 1991 when John Major and Douglas Hurd went to Maastricht to negotiate a new European Treaty, they were warned by Eurosceptics such as the Home Secretary Michael Howard that if the Treaty was in any sense federal or if it committed the UK to the Social Chapter which includes rights for workers such as maternity pay for women working part-time, than there would be resignations.

Major and Hurd managed to negotiate a Treaty which satisfied the Eurosceptics. The opt-outs on the Social Chapter and on EMU, plus the removal of the word 'federal' from the Treaty were enough to keep the party relatively united, allowing it to go on to win the April 1992 General Election against the odds.

The Tory majority was slashed from 101 in June 1987 to 21 in 1992, but even so the Tories were elated by their fourth consecutive victory, and reduced interest rates to 10 per cent. No party at that election opposed the Maastricht Treaty – indeed, Europe barely featured as an issue, itself a reflection of Major's ability to defuse the tensions within his party. In retrospect it could be said that Major made a tactical error in not pushing Maastricht through Parliament in the summer of 1992 while he was enjoying a post-election honeymoon.

RATIFYING THE MAASTRICHT TREATY

By the end of June 1992, the British had assumed the presidency of the European Community. John Major should have been in a formidably powerful position, but the result of the Danish referendum of June 1992 where the people voted against the Maastricht Treaty, gave new heart to the British opponents of Maastricht. The stage was set for a battle between Baroness Thatcher's 'government in exile' and the Major-Hurd forces.

There were over 200 hours of debate over the Maastricht Treaty in the Commons, and over 600 amendments. In the early stages of the battle the sceptics refrained from attacking Major directly, after all he had recently delivered election victory. The object of their derision was Douglas Hurd. Richard Ryder, the Tory Chief Whip, and Tristan Garel-Jones, a junior Minister at the Foreign Office, had to steer the bill through the Commons, knowing that rejection of Maastricht by any single nation would invalidate the whole Treaty. All three party leaderships wanted the treaty to be ratified, but all had to manoeuvre to placate their own party rebels.

At the Tory Party Conference of October 1992, Hurd reminded his party of the dangers of division, using the analogy of 1846 when the party had split over the repeal of the Corn Laws. Academics also cited the divisions of 1903, when the Conservative Party was divided over Imperial Preference (preferential treatment for trade with countries of the Empire), as evidence of the damage inflicted by splits.

The Maastricht Paving Bill was passed on November 4th by just three votes, with 26 Conservatives voting against and six abstaining. The following day, the government announced that it would delay ratification until after the second Danish referendum on the Maastricht Treaty.

THE EDINBURGH SUMMIT DECEMBER 1992

This summit granted opt-out arrangements to Denmark, and also underlined the importance of subsidiarity – a Declaration on Subsidiarity aimed to persuade the Danish people and the British Eurosceptics to accept the Maastricht Treaty. The problem was disagreement over the definition of subsidiarity. Following the Maastricht Treaty, the British had used subsidiarity as an argument for leaving as much decision-making as possible to national governments. Other European countries regarded it as a way of devolving power down to regional and local authorities. This was never going to sit easily with a Conservative government which since 1979 had reduced the powers of local authorities, and totally opposed devolution for Scotland and Wales.

TROUBLES WITH PARLIAMENT

The British government had claimed that if the opt-out on the Social Chapter was deleted, the Treaty would be invalidated and all 12 states would have to return to the drawing board. The government implied that it could ratify the Treaty by using the royal prerogative, thereby bypassing the need for Parliament's approval. Then in February of 1993 the government did a U-turn with Hurd claiming that rejecting the protocol to the bill, which excludes the Social Chapter, actually would not in itself bring the Social Chapter in.

Ratifying the Treaty became a personal test of strength for John Major's leadership, and the third reading on May 20th was passed by 292 to 212. At the Copenhagen Summit of late June 1993, Major rejected Delors' attempt to launch a Community-wide onslaught on unemployment. This was exactly what the British sceptics wanted from Major. He also reassured them by replacing Garel-Jones with the sceptic David Heathcoat-Amory.

In July, William Rees Mogg, a former Editor of *The Times* and now a Life Peer, applied to the High Court for a judicial review of the government's right to ratify the Treaty. However, the crucial moment came on July 22nd when Tory rebels joined with Labour and the Liberal Democrats in a vote over the Social Chapter. In what Major described as a 'cynical and unscrupulous vote' the government was defeated by 324 to 316; Ludlum called it 'the worst Commons defeat on a Conservative government this century'. Major threatened to call an election if this was not immediately reversed. The government won the vote of confidence on July 23rd by 339 to 299, but the very fact that just 15 months after an election victory the Prime Minister was having to call a vote of confidence in his own government, was an indication of the mess the party was in.

On August 1st 1993, the ERM was effectively suspended. Rees Mogg took the view that this rendered all talk of EMU superfluous and dropped his challenge in the courts the following day – the same day that the Maastricht Treaty was finally ratified.

MAJOR'S CONTINUING 'LOCAL DIFFICULTIES'

In 1958 responding to the resignation of his Chancellor and the entire Treasury team, the Prime Minister, Harold Macmillan had claimed that this represented a 'little local difficulty'. During the three years following Maastricht, the Conservative Party was in a state of open conflict over Europe, a conflict that really did make Macmillan's earlier difficulties look miniscule. John Major sacked his Chancellor, Norman Lamont in May 1993. His former friend and supporter did not go willingly, and his resignation speech was a blistering attack on the incompetence of the administration. He became a fierce backbench critic and a focus of discontent. Lamont began to discuss openly the possibility of the UK pulling out of the EU.

More importantly, the Conservative Party itself was now dividing into factions, a very unusual spectacle. Of course the party has always contained a diversity of views, from the pro- and anti-appeasement divisions of the 1930s, to the divisions over the dismantling of Empire in the 1960s. However throughout most of its history the party has remained relatively united, hence the talk of unity as the party's secret weapon. Divisions have tended to be between tendencies (loose informal groupings), rather than factions which have a clear structure. The divisions of the 1990s were much more ideological and partisan.

At the 1994 local elections, the Tories polled just 27 per cent, virtually the same as the Liberal Democrats. Major had to tread a difficult path seeking to balance the different factions.

Major and Hurd called for a 'variable geometry' which would allow some member states to proceed with more integration; eg, six of the Schengen countries announced that they would remove all internal border controls, while the UK, Ireland and Denmark would not. However, what Major saw as a 'multi-speed, multi-track, multi-layered Europe', Labour and the Liberal Democrats interpreted as a willingness to condemn Britain to a 'European second division', a 'Club Med' group including Greece and Portugal, while a Nordic 'superleague' led by Germany and France surged ahead.

On occasions Major would appear to adopt a more Eurosceptic stance; eg:

- he refused to budge over QMV in the run up to the Corfu Summit in Spring 1994, which would discuss the implications of enlargement.
- he threatened to disrupt EU business unless the ban on British beef was lifted.

Such stances were intended to endear him more to the sceptic wing of his party, and to those sections of the press which were increasingly strident in their hostility to the EU such as the Murdoch-owned *The Sun* and *The Times*.

The Corfu Summit, 1994

At the Corfu summit in late June 1994, John Major vetoed the appointment of Jean-Luc Dehaene as President of the Commission. Deheane was a Belgian federalist, a Christian Democrat and therefore well to the left of most Tories. The Germans had already blocked the appointment of the Dutch Prime Minister Ruud Lubbers, and Deheane was seen as Helmut Kohl's candidate. It was the 'turn' of the Benelux countries to supply the President, so eventually Jacques Santer was given the job. Major's stance won support from the Eurosceptics but provoked hostility from Heath – 'the more you try to please the Eurosceptics the more they will demand.'

THE 1994 EUROPEAN ELECTIONS

In the European election campaign, John Major talked of his belief in a 'two speed Europe'. In the 1994 European elections Labour won 64 of the UK's 87 seats to the Conservative's 18. This made British Labour the largest group in the European Parliament, and represented the worst ever national performance for the Tories – just 28 per cent of the votes, whereas Labour polled 45 per cent of the votes. However, this was not quite as bad as had been feared for the Tories, and avoidance of 'meltdown' gave Major a breathing space. He was able to postpone a leadership election, which would have been highly embarrassing at that time given the recent death of John Smith, the Labour Party leader, in May 1994.

The turn out for these elections was just 36.1 per cent, a mere 4 per cent up on the first direct elections in 1979. The average for the member states was 57 per cent. This is much lower than the average in British General Elections, but still higher than Presidential elections in the USA.

THE WHIP COMES OFF

At the Conservative Conference of autumn 1994, delegates were indignant at the behaviour of the Commission and the demands of the EU in general. At a fringe meeting, Norman Lamont raised the issue of withdrawal from the EU. Douglas Hurd warned the conference against 'getting a little high on xenophobia' but it was Michael Portillo's call to 'stop the rot from Brussels' which warmed the delegates.

On November 28th, the Commons voted on the government bill to increase the amount of cash going to the EU. John Major made it into a vote of confidence, and eight Conservative MPs who abstained, had the whip withdrawn; ie, they were excluded from the Parliamentary Conservative Party. Another Tory dissident relinquished the whip in sympathy with the eight. Forty Labour MPs voted against the government rather than abstain, but the bill was passed. Eurosceptic Tories challenged the Chairman of the Conservative backbench committee (the 1922 Committee) Sir Marcus Fox, putting forward the sceptic Nicholas Bonsor to challenge him, because in their eyes Fox had been too supportive of the government over the European bill.

Divisions within the Cabinet periodically resurfaced, in particular over EMU. By April 1995 the whipless rebels had been readmitted to the fold without making a single concession. According to Ian Aitken 'rarely in living memory has a chief whip (not to mention his Prime Minister who acted in his advice) been so utterly humiliated'.

This increased the possibility of a leadership challenge to John Major, and even many Eurosceptics were beginning to look at the pro-European Michael Heseltine favourably in the hope that he would minimise the Conservative losses at the next election and then make way for their favourite, Michael Portillo. There had been no leadership challenge in 1994 because of the reasons mentioned on p. 78, and also because of the failure of the dissidents to get the backing of the necessary ten per cent of Tory MPs to mount a challenge. However, Major was far from secure in his position, and his refusal to rule out the possibility of the UK entering into EMU was one factor behind this.

THE CONSERVATIVE LEADERSHIP ELECTION OF 1995

In a surprise move in June 1995, John Major resigned his position as party leader, and challenged his party to 'put up or shut up'. His strategy may have been that if a challenger was put up, it would be a backbencher such as Norman Lamont. Frontbenchers would feel bound by collective responsibility, and would therefore back the Prime Minister. To Major's dismay, one of his Cabinet, the Welsh Secretary and former Thatcher adviser John Redwood resigned and took up Major's challenge. He told the party that 'no change of leadership would mean no chance at the next election', and was supported by many prominent sceptics such as Teresa Gorman and Tony Marlow.

It was always unlikely that Redwood could defeat Major, but it was possible that Major would be so wounded that he would withdraw after a first inconclusive ballot (as Edward Heath had done in 1975 and Margaret Thatcher had done in 1990), leaving the way clear for Cabinet Ministers such as Michael Heseltine and Michael Portillo to enter. This would then provide the party with a straight fight between Euroenthusiastic Heseltine and Eurosceptic Portillo.

However Major did a deal with Heseltine, whereby the latter was appointed Deputy Prime Minister, with a key role in coordinating government; in return, Heseltine's supporters backed Major. Major survived the first ballot, but about one-third of his party had failed to vote for him. It was felt by many in other European governments that Major was still the prisoner of his critics, and that he would be increasingly obstructive. This meant they wanted to delay the IGC in the hope of a change of government in Britain.

The aftermath

Douglas Hurd was replaced as Foreign Secretary by the Defence Secretary Malcolm Rifkind, who began to sound more cautious over Europe, and the sceptics felt that they had won the argument. Rifkind identified Europe as 'the new fault line of British politics'. At the 1995 conference, Norman Lamont said, 'we are all Eurosceptics now'. Michael Portillo made a speech attacking Brussels and asserting Britain's sovereign control over her defence forces. He was clearly anxious to re-establish his credentials with the sceptic right, after John Redwood had apparently taken on the role of leader of the Thatcherites in the leadership election, but even so, the crassness of the speech rebounded on Portillo. He was now given the difficult job of Secretary of Defence, at a time of defence cuts.

After the Tory leadership election John Major managed to marginalise the hard core Eurosceptics within the Cabinet, and unite most of the party behind a populist nationalist anti-European rhetoric. The Chancellor Kenneth Clarke deplored it, but it appeared to work.

RUN-UP TO THE 1997 GENERAL ELECTION

In March 1996 the Government published a White Paper, *A Partnership of Nations*, setting out its negotiating position for the IGC. It was intended to unite the party behind a broadly sceptical stance, but the cracks remained very visible and the defection of Tory MP Emma Nicholson in December 1995 to the Liberal Democrats pointed the warning that if Major went too far towards the Eurosceptics, other pro-European Tory MPs might follow Nicholson's example. Despite rumours of ten Tory MPs defecting to the Liberal Democrats, no more Tories crossed the floor, but many pro-European Tory MPs chose to stand down at the 1997 General Election. This meant that, win or lose, the party would most likely shift to a more sceptical stance.

There was talk that around 30 Tory MPs such as Peter Temple-Morris, and members of the Tory Reform Group, were discussing ways in which they could cooperate with a future Labour government under Tony Blair. John Redwood appeared to hesitate when asked whether a Eurosceptic voter should support the Referendum Party rather than the Tories in the election. At the same time, former Euroenthusiasts such as Stephen Dorrel were making sceptic noises, perhaps in an attempt to curry favour with the Tory right, should a leadership election follow general election defeat. Two months before the election Dorrel was breaking with Cabinet ranks over EMU, by coming out in favour of it. (In fact it was all to backfire on him, because in the Tory leadership election of summer 1997, he failed to get support even on the left of the party. He was punished for being too openly ambitious and opportunistic.)

In November 1996, John Major once more antagonised Eurosceptic backbenchers by refusing to allow a debate on the stability pact, the German idea for enforcing financial discipline after EMU. He appeared to withhold vital information from MPs, but under pressure, he backed down and a two-day debate ensued. However, at the same time, he announced that he would veto the outcome of the IGC unless the ECJ ruling against Britain on the Working Time Directive was overturned. With his past record on backing down after issuing threats (he had done so in 1994 over QMV and 1996 over the beef crisis), the *Daily Mail* asked, 'does he mean it this time?'

THE 1997 BRITISH GENERAL ELECTION

Opinion polls since Black Wednesday (September 16th 1992) had shown the Tory Party heading for a landslide defeat, a prognosis endorsed by all the local elections and by-election results from 1993 onwards and by the 1994 European elections. Even so, the scale of the Labour landslide victory took almost everyone by surprise. It is difficult if not impossible to establish for certain the causes of the Tory disaster, the worst since 1906. Commentators always say that elections in the UK never revolve around just one issue, and certainly 1997 was no exception. A record number of Cabinet Ministers lost their seats, including Eurosceptics such as Michael Portillo, Euroenthusiasts such as David Hunt, and those who tried to steer a middle course such as Malcolm Rifkind. Voters appeared ready to punish Conservative candidates irrespective of their views on Europe. There were concerns about the Tory record on tax and sleaze, there were questions marks about Major's leadership, and there was definitely a feeling that after 18 years it was time for change.

In the immediate aftermath of defeat, Tories pointed to the abstention of people who would normally vote Tory, and the fact that other natural supporters were lured away by James Goldsmith. However the Referendum Party may not have damaged the Conservatives as much as some believe; indeed it may well have prevented Labour from winning certain seats because the anti-Tory vote went to Goldsmith's party rather than Labour. It may be that the UK Independence Party was more of a threat to the Tories. However, when all these considerations are taken into account, there is no doubt that the Tory divisions over Europe had damaged the party very seriously just as Hurd had warned they would. Perhaps the election really was lost on September 16th 1992.

THE TORY PARTY UNDER WILLIAM HAGUE

On May 2nd 1997, John Major resigned as leader of the Conservative Party. Michael Heseltine had ongoing problems with his health so he would not stand, and Michael Portillo, President of the Board of Trade, Ian Lang and Malcolm Rifkind had lost their seats, so they could not. Several prominent Tories put themselves forward, Eurosceptics John Redwood, Michael Howard and Peter Lilley, and Euroenthusiasts Kenneth Clarke and Stephen Dorrel (although he soon withdrew and endorsed Clarke). There was talk of William Hague endorsing Michael Howard, but 'the dream ticket' fell apart when Hague decided to run for the leadership.

The candidate's stances on Europe rapidly emerged as a major issue. By the second ballot, it was down to the sceptics William Hague and John Redwood versus the Euroenthusiast Kenneth Clarke. It was widely felt that Clarke was the heavyweight of the party, backed by the Conservative Constituency Associations; he was enormously experienced, populist and feared by the Labour Party, but simply too pro-Europe for the Parliamentary Conservative Party of the late 1990s. Redwood was forced out in the second ballot and in a surprise move, made an agreement with Clarke. They would agree to disagree over EMU. This backfired and provoked a 'stop Clarke' campaign, with Margaret Thatcher strongly endorsing Hague, who won on the third ballot. He promised a free vote on EMU and stated that his view was that Britain should not join for the *foreseeable future.*

Clarke refused to join Hague's Shadow Cabinet but all the other candidates did so. By the party conference in the autumn of 1997, the leadership was toughening its anti-European stance, declaring British membership of ERM to have been a mistake. In the weeks that followed, the Shadow Cabinet changed its 'no to EMU for the foreseeable future' to 'no for the next ten years', in other words, two parliaments. This provoked the resignation of shadow government spokesman Ian Taylor and of a Shadow Cabinet member David Currie, as well as the eventual defection to Labour by the backbencher Peter Temple-Morris; defiant speeches from Heseltine and Clarke encouraged pro-European Conservatives to stay and fight the European cause from within the party. Tory MPs were instructed to vote against the Amsterdam Treaty in June, the first time the party had ever officially opposed a European Treaty.

In an attempt to display strong leadership in mid-November 1997, the Tory whips ejected Temple-Morris from the Parliamentary Party, a move condemned by Heseltine and fellow Euroenthusiasts. This coincided with a landslide Tory defeat in the Winchester by-election when a Liberal Democrat majority of two was turned into one of over 20,000, making it the safest Liberal Democrat seat in the country; and near humiliation in the Beckenham by-election when a normally safe Tory seat was won by just over 1,000 votes. The candidate's stance on Europe appears not to have been an issue; the new Tory MP for Beckenham is actually a close adviser of William Hague.

CONCLUSION

By the CBI conference in November 1997, the moderately Euroenthusiastic Labour Chancellor Gordon Brown appeared to be closer to the business community than William Hague. Indeed for the first time this century, there appeared every prospect of a rift between the Conservatives and the business world. This is simply the logical culmination of the tensions within the post-1975 (when Margaret Thatcher became leader and the party shifted to the right) Conservative Party.

Thatcherism combined a nationalist political stance with free market economic policies. Where she was willing to concede authority politically, it was to the United States rather than to Europe, and it was over defence issues. The only serious rift between the Thatcher governments and the USA came in 1983 when the USA invaded the Caribbean island of Grenada to overthrow its Marxist regime. It did so without consulting the UK, even though it was a former British colony and still in the Commonwealth. On every other major issue (the Falklands, the 1986 US bombing of Libya from British bases, the Gulf War of 1990/91), London was in full sympathy with Washington. However, if the European Community attempted to move from a free trade zone to 'ever closer union', this brought out the nationalist instincts within the Thatcherites even where the British business community was largely persuaded of the need for integration. This was as true of ERM in the 1980s as it was to be of EMU in the 1990s.

According to William Wallace 'the Conservative Party loses its head most completely when its sense of English identity is thrown into confusion', which is why it is so opposed to devolution for Scotland and Wales, and to any weakening of the Union with Northern Ireland. All are seen as threatening the integrity of the United Kingdom. An even greater threat is offered by what some Tories see as the federalist ambitions of the EU. Speaking at The Hague in 1992, *The Guardian* reported Margaret Thatcher as asking whether Europe

'is to be a tightly regulated, centralised bureaucratic federal state imposing uniform standards upon the Continent? Or is it to be a loose knit decentralised free market of sovereign states, based upon competition between different national systems of tax and regulation within a free trade area?'

John Major constantly tried to balance the different wings of the party in an attempt to prove that it could be a 'broad church' over Europe. The Tory leadership of the late 1990s adopted the Thatcherite vision, knowing that this will alienate some sections of the party, but hoping that clarity of policy will impress the voters.

Leading Tory MPs such as David Willets, a former adviser to Margaret Thatcher and one of the party's foremost intellectuals, oppose further integration, because they argue since 1979 the UK and the rest of the Union have diverged. Thatcherism has succeeded in 'rolling back the state', whereas on the Continent even rightwing regimes such as Kohl's in Germany and Chirac's in France are more statist. In 1979 the state accounted for about 45 per cent of GNP in Britain and on the Continent. By 1997, that figure was down to 40 per cent in Britain and up to 50 per cent in Europe.

LABOUR AND EUROPE

It would be a grave mistake to think that the Labour Party is somehow immune from divisions and confusion over the European issue. Quite the opposite is true: the party was extremely divided over Europe in the 1970s and early 1980s. Divisions over Europe were a crucial factor in the weakening of the Labour Party in the 1970s and early 1980s, leading to the resignation of the one time Deputy Leader of the Party, Roy Jenkins, and helping to bring about the split in the party in 1981 which arguably helped perpetuate Tory rule.

THE SOCIAL DEMOCRATIC PARTY

Until 1975 Labour refused to take its seats in the European Parliament. The 1980 Labour Party Conference had voted for British withdrawal from the Community. In 1981, Roy Jenkins returned to British politics, and together with three other former Labour Cabinet Ministers, Shirley Williams, David Owen and Bill Rodgers (collectively known as the Gang Of Four), he set up the Social Democratic Party (SDP) in 1981. They had broken away from the Labour Party because they said it had moved too far to the left on a whole range of issues including defence, internal party reform and Europe. According to the former Labour MP and founder member of the SDP, David Marquand 'Labour's commitment to withdraw from the EC was the most important single symbol of its lurch to old-style fundamentalism'. The SDP formed an electoral pact with the pro-European Liberal Party and at the 1983 election, with Labour fighting on a programme which included a pledge to take the country out of Europe (a pledge which Tony Benn described as the most crucial policy plank), the SDP-Liberal Alliance polled just 700,000 votes less than Labour, although the electoral system saw the Alliance win just 23 seats to Labour's 209.

Yet by the 1988 Labour Conference the party recognised 'that Britain is politically and economically integrated in the European Community'. Things had come a long way since the days when the Community was derided by socialists as a 'capitalist club', the 'rich West end of Europe defended against the poor East end by NATO'. One factor in the changed perception was the enlargement of the

Community to include Southern Mediterranean states such as Greece (admitted in 1981), Portugal and Spain (admitted in 1986). These nations were both relatively poor and also had socialist governments. Another major development was that Mikhail Gorbachev, having come to power in the USSR in 1986, was attempting to reform the economy (*perestroika*) and open up the political system (*glasnost*) at the same time as easing superpower tensions and referring to Europe as 'our common home'. The old certainties of a divided continent were ending.

Labour and the British unions were simply coming into line with their European counterparts. Labour agreed to fight the 1989 European elections on the common European socialist manifesto; in Marquand's words 'explicitly assenting to the future development of the EC'. The manifesto stressed economic democracy and social rights. Its central themes were solidarity, social cohesion and a citizen's Europe. The journalist John Lloyd commented on 'the speed and painlessness' with which Labour's turn around was accomplished. In his view it was not a product of a shift to Europe but part of the excision of socialism from the party, its move from democratic socialism to social democracy.

Democratic socialism as expounded by people like Tony Benn, involves a much greater degree of state intervention in the economy while *social democracy*, which accepts a predominantly private sector economy. Britain's Labour Party had since 1918 been theoretically committed to democratic socialism via clause (iv) of its constitution, which envisaged 'public ownership of the means of production, distribution and exchange'. In practice, Labour governments had never sought to implement the clause in its entirety, and had been content with nationalising the 'commanding heights' of the economy such as coal and the railways. The Labour Party leader 1983–92, Neil Kinnock distanced Labour from Bennite ideas, and Europe provided a useful vehicle for this move.

European socialist parties had long since moved away from democratic socialism.

- In Germany, the Social Democratic Party had renounced it in 1959 and had subsequently been much more electorally successful, sharing power in some form from 1966 to 1982.
- The French socialists had won the Presidency for the first time in 1981 on a leftwing platform, and François Mitterand had originally had Communists in his government, but by 1983 he had dismissed the Communists and shifted to the centre.
- The Portuguese, Spanish and Greek socialists, and outside of Europe, the Australian and New Zealand Labour Parties, had all similarly moved away from old style state interventionism.
- Even the Chinese and Soviet Communists were experimenting with free market ideas by the 1980s.

Neil Kinnock's party was now following suit.

By 1992, Labour had lost four consecutive elections to the Conservatives. The party was demoralised and divided. Kinnock resigned, and with the Electoral College still dominated by the Unions, it was clear that the new leader would be the former Shadow Chancellor John Smith, despite the fact that some in the party blamed his 'shadow budget' of early 1992 for the party's defeat. Smith was cautious and argued against radical policy changes. He believed that the party would return to power at the next election, after 'one more heave'. This belief was confirmed in his eyes when the new Major government ran into trouble over Maastricht, ERM and pit closures. The major Shadow Cabinet casualty of the Smith era was the sceptic Bryan Gould, once tipped as a future leader, who in Autumn 1992 resigned from Labour's front bench because he opposed their support for ERM. He soon left British politics altogether, another indication that Labour was becoming more and more pro-Europe.

John Smith was one of the Labour rebels of 1971, who by voting for entry to the EEC, had saved the Prime Minister Edward Heath from his own rebels. Arguably Smith could have brought John Major down, had Labour voted against the Maastricht Treaty, but once more he chose to save a Conservative government from defeat. Labour's objections to the Treaty were only that it did not go far enough, ie, it did not include the Social Chapter. Sixty-one Labour MPs defied the whips to vote against the second reading of the Maastricht bill in 1993.

By 1993, Labour was well ahead in the polls and the Conservatives were suffering spectacular local and by-election defeats. The only major change pushed through by John Smith was a reform of the Electoral College to elect Labour's leader. The new system, agreed at the 1993 conference, would involve one member one vote (OMOV) within each of the three sections of the party. No one expected at that stage that the party would be using the new system in less than six months, as it was plunged into another leadership election caused by the sudden death of John Smith in May 1994.

THE ARRIVAL OF TONY BLAIR

The Labour campaign to elect John Smith's successor did not take place until after the European elections of June 1994, out of respect for him. It resulted in the landslide victory of Tony Blair, who defeated John Prescott and Margaret Becket. Blair won convincing majorities in all three sections (MPs, affiliated bodies such as Trade Unions and individual members of constituency parties), and could portray his mandate as overwhelming.

Before his death, John Smith had been labelled the 'poodle of Brussels' by John Major. Blair was unwilling to let Major portray him as too soft on Europe. In turn this increased the pressure on Major to take a more sceptic stance.

From the mid-1980s Labour grew keener on Europe. By the late 1980s and 1990s, even the leftwing of the party was far more willing to concede that the possibility of a British government independently introducing socialism was remote. As the former leftwing backbencher (currently a Labour Minister) Peter Hain argued, business and finance operate at a global level 'yet there are no democratic mechanisms to exert a countervailing influence on behalf of the people'. The implication is that the days when any nation state could act on its own are over; there can no longer be 'socialism in one country', so Britain should join with its European partners in creating democratically accountable European political mechanisms.

However, even by the late 1990s there were significant forces and individuals within the party who were sceptical about further integration. Sceptics such as Peter Shore, Austen Mitchell and Tony Benn often made common cause with their fellow disbelievers in the Tory Party. However, the divisions were not as politically damaging because:

1   Labour was not in power and therefore not having to make policy decisions on an ongoing basis.
2   The divisions did not appear to go up to Shadow Cabinet level, although it was well known that Gordon Brown was more enthusiastic about EMU than Robin Cook and John Prescott, both former anti-marketeers.
3   The defence of national sovereignty is an intrinsically more sensitive issue for the avowedly nationalist Conservative Party than for the supposedly more internationalist Labour Party.

Labour had taken a step back from its Euroenthusiasm of the early 1990s after Robin Cook took over from John Cunningham as Shadow Foreign Secretary in 1994. Cook spent his first year in this post repositioning Labour on Europe. With Labour moving away from Euroenthusiasm for electoral reasons, there was a narrowing of policy differences, except on the Social Chapter, between Labour and the Clarke faction of Tories.

At the same time, Tony Blair persuaded the party to do what Hugh Gaitskell (Labour leader 1955–1963) had been unable to do in 1960 and Neil Kinnock had not even dared to attempt – the dropping of clause (iv). This was a sign of Blair's power within the party, of his determination to create 'New Labour', and yet more evidence of Labour's movement towards European style social democracy. By early 1996 he was talking of a 'stakeholding' economy which, although he was careful to be ambiguous, appeared to mean a German-style social market approach in which companies have wider responsibilities than simply making the maximum profit for their shareholders.

The Centre for European Reform was founded in 1995 to campaign for a ten point programme to improve understanding of the work of the European Union. Robin Cook addressed the body in February 1997 arguing that British prosperity depended upon vigorous and constructive engagement with the EU.

THE LABOUR LANDSLIDE

At the election of May 1st 1997, Labour won 419 out of 659 seats, giving them an overall majority of 179, the biggest in the postwar period. The number of Tory MPs had halved, indeed the Labour majority was bigger than the total number of Tory MPs. On most issues, Labour could probably look to support from the 46 Liberal Democrat MPs, so provided party loyalty held, their position in the Commons looked impregnable.

THE LABOUR GOVERNMENT AND EUROPE

With Labour now in power, a majority of EU member states had left-of-centre governments. The last time Labour was in power there were not even direct elections to the European Parliament and British politics was still relatively unaffected by the Community. Now there was no doubt that the biggest issues facing the new government were European.

French President Jacques Chirac was facing such difficulties in getting the French economy to conform to the Maastricht Treaty criteria, that he decided to hold parliamentary elections in 1997, a year early, in the hope of receiving a renewed mandate. Instead, the French Socialists under Lionel Jospin recovered from their very poor performance in 1993 and defeated the rightwing government of Alain Juppé. The victory of the French socialists also enhanced the power of the left within the European Union. However, the politics of Europe have never been about a straightforward left-right divide, and Blair's New Labour appeared to have little in common with Jospin's socialists.

The Socialists are the biggest grouping in the European Parliament, only because the British electoral system of first-past-the-post distorts outcomes, giving Labour 62 seats in the 1994 European elections on share of the vote. Many Blairite MPs believe Labour MEPs such as Ken Coates to be 'Old Labour' and therefore an embarrassment. The Blair government has decided to contest the 1999 European elections on a list system of PR. This has led to rows within the Labour Party, because it will reduce the number of Labour MEPs by about 20, and because list systems centralise power within the party. List systems are used in Italy, France and Spain, which also have relatively low turn outs for perhaps that very reason.

Even though Labour moved to a more Euroenthusiastic stance in the late 1980s, we should not over-estimate Labour's willingness to pursue integration. The supposedly charismatic Tony Blair is so concerned about appearing too pro-European for the British public that, despite presiding over a buoyant economy that could easily meet the Maastricht criteria, having a majority of 179 and facing a Tory Party in disarray, he is unwilling to forfeit the support of the Murdoch press and risk a referendum rebuff on EMU until after he is safely returned to power in 2002 (or whenever the next General Election is called). Blair is clearly a long way removed from the more integrationist Oskar Lafontaine of the German Socialists, or Lionel Jospin the French Socialist Prime Minister, or the Italian Socialists.

THE LIBERAL DEMOCRATS

The only party that can realistically claim to be more or less united over Europe is the Liberal Democrat Party. Ever since the late 1950s, under a succession of leaders (Joe Grimond, Jeremy Thorpe, David Steel and now Paddy Ashdown), the Liberal Democrats have been consistently supportive of European integration. There are only a handful of Liberal Democrats who are sceptical over Europe. The official party position is in favour of a federal Europe.

Cynics might argue that Liberal Democrat enthusiasm for all things European is because they have no hope of achieving power domestically, and therefore have nothing to fear from a surrender of power to Brussels. However, to be fair to the party, their stance on Europe is part of a broader, more coherent strategy of devolving power from Westminster, involving:

- devolution both to Scotland and Wales but also to the regions of England
- proportional representation for elections to revived local authorities, the Assemblies of Scotland and Wales, the European Parliament, the newly elected upper chamber at Westminster as well as the Commons itself
- incorporation of the European Declaration of Rights as a British Bill of Rights superior to statute law
- a genuinely strong and accountable system of local government.

This should all be guaranteed by a codified constitution interpreted by a British version of the American Supreme Court.

Liberal Democrats are the true believers in subsidiarity, arguing for a Europe of the Regions in which some power would go upwards to Brussels, but much power would be devolved downwards, bypassing the nation state altogether. The party leader in the Lords is Lord Roy Jenkins (the former Labour Chancellor and Home Secretary who broke with Labour in the early 1970s when it switched to a Eurosceptic stance). Tony Blair is an open admirer of Jenkins, who now chairs the Blair-appointed Commission on electoral reform. Liberal Democrat leader Paddy Ashdown sits on a Cabinet Committee on constitutional reform, so Liberal Democrat influence on New Labour is plain to see, and may well push them in a more pro-European direction.

SUMMARY

It is clear that all three major British political parties have been deeply affected by European integration. Both Labour and the Conservatives have been split on the issue which seems to transcend the standard left-right political axis. This has brought about some strange political alignments such as that in the 1975 referendum campaign. The Liberals are more united over Europe but have been unable to influence British government policy except briefly in the late 1970s and perhaps again now in the late 1990s.

British politics is based on strong party loyalty. Indeed, this is one of the aspects of the British system which may be said to account for British 'awkwardness' in Europe where party loyalty tends to be weaker. It could be that European integration may ultimately force a major realignment of the British party system. There are already signs that it is doing that as pro-European Conservatives break away.

| STUDY | GUIDES |

Revision Hints

For many people, politics is about parties, and their understanding of the European issue is a product of their awareness of how it has divided both the major parties. Your notes need to bring out clearly the nature of those divisions over the last four decades, so again it is important to refer back to the historical chapters.

It is useful to look at each of the parties separately, but at the same time to be aware that each party affects the others, so that for example part of the reason why the Labour Party switched its approach towards Europe by 1988, was the impact of developments within the Conservative Party.

In the case of the Labour Party, the divisions over Europe had a very dramatic impact on the party from the moment it lost office in 1970 to the point at which Labour switched to a more enthusiastic stance in the second half of the 1980s. You need to be aware of the reasons behind the change of approach, as well as of the remaining divisions within the party.

Your notes need to trace the same divisions and tensions within the Conservative Party, in particular the way in which the European issue became bound up with the role of the leadership. You should consider why it is that the Liberal Democrats have appeared so united over European issues.

The following essays both deal with divisions within the main parties.

1 To what extent were arguments within the Conservative Party over Europe from 1986 onwards really arguments about the leadership and the direction of the party?

2 'Labour learned to love Europe simply because Thatcher fell out with it'. Discuss.

Both essays require you to look at the divisions within the two major parties over recent years and relate them to the rows over Europe. The clear implication in both cases is that Europe was a scapegoat, the Tories were fighting over Europe when the real issue was the domination of Thatcher and the resistance to the ERM. This meant that by 1990, John Major took over a thoroughly divided party. It continued to argue over issues which appeared more and more obscure to the British public, such as whether to rule EMU out or to wait and see, or, if it was to be ruled out, was that for the foreseeable future or for ten years? However, your essay needs to balance this by looking at ways in which Europe really did create an ideological divide within the party, as a choice had to be made between economic internationalism and political nationalism.

The second essay covers similar ground but from the perspective of the left. You need to consider ways in which Labour's embracing of all things European was simply a tactical ploy, versus ways in which the conversion of Labour was a belated recognition that British socialism needed to become more like European social democracy.

Although neither essay question mentions the Liberal Democrats, you could still use them as a point of comparison and contrast. Why were the other two parties divided over Europe when the Liberal Democrats stayed united? Was it something in the ideology of liberalism which accepted federalism, or was it simply that the Liberal Democrats have not been in power and therefore not had to make difficult decisions threatening party unity?

As with some of the other essays a useful start would be two columns with reasons for and against the argument in each of them.

1 'Both main parties have been split by Europe and will continue to be so.' How valid is this view?
2 Why are the Liberal Democrats so enthusiastic over European integration?

6

PRESSURE GROUPS AND EUROPE

Introduction

THIS CHAPTER CONSIDERS the impact of Europe upon British pressure groups. A pressure group is an organisation, either ad hoc or permanent, which does not put forward candidates for election but seeks to influence those in power, either at local, national or international levels. British pressure groups have been adjusting to a world in which policies that most concern them are often decided upon in Brussels. Therefore, regardless of their views on European integration, if they wish to have some input into the policy-making process they need to lobby not just the British government, but also the institutions of the EU. We can illustrate the changed role for pressure groups by looking in detail at five policy areas: the environment, the Social Chapter of the Maastricht Treaty, EMU, farming and fishing, and the BSE crisis.

Key Points
This chapter contains material on the following key issues:

- The nature of policy-making within the European Union.
- The way in which Europe has shaped the world which pressure groups inhabit, through reference to issues such as the environment.
- The impact Europe has had on the two sides of British industry: employers and employees.
- How Europe has affected British agriculture and fishing.

THE EFFECT ON PRESSURE GROUPS

Pressure groups are like political parties in that they are both instruments for mobilising bias, bringing together like-minded people who wish to change something or prevent something being changed. There are often very close relationships between parties and pressure groups. The Labour Party was created in 1900 by, among other organisations, the trade unions, who hoped to exercise political influence beneficial to their members by securing representation in Parliament. The unions still form the industrial wing of the Labour movement. However, there are important differences between parties and pressure groups:

- Parties seek power; pressure groups should, in a liberal democracy, confine themselves to seeking influence, otherwise they can be seen as illegitimate.
- Parties tend to have policies on a broad range of issues; pressure groups may well be single-issue organisations, as with the Campaign for Lead Free Petrol.

In the nineteenth century, the classic days of the sovereign nation state, there was relatively little need for pressure groups to operate across national frontiers. When business became international in the twentieth century then workers' movements had to follow, but it has only really been in the postwar period that we have seen the creation of more and more intergovernmental and supranational organisations, from the General Agreement on Tariff and Trade (GATT – now the World Trade Organisation), the International Monetary Fund (IMF) and the World Bank, to the European Free Trade Association (EFTA), the European Union and the European Economic Area. As such intergovernmental bodies have become more important, so pressure groups have had to lobby at international level.

PRESSURE GROUPS IN THE EU

The Council of Ministers meets in Brussels, with most of the work done by bureaucrats (about 90 per cent of decisions are taken before Ministers get involved). Pressure groups tend to lobby the officials rather than the Council of Ministers directly, in exactly the same way as within the British political system – insider groups tend to lobby the bureaucrats who are permanent, rather than the Ministers who are temporary. In terms of British government, the Departments of Trade, Agriculture, Defence, the Treasury and the Foreign Office are most intimately involved in European politics, but increasingly almost every aspect of government activity is touched. Equally in terms of pressure groups, the producer groups, business organisations, the farmers and the trade unions together with certain promotional groups such as Greenpeace and Commission World Farming are most involved in European issues.

The Treaty of Rome set up an Economic and Social Committee (ESC) to provide a voice for the various economic and social interests of member states. Prior to the most recent enlargement it had 189 members, 24 from the UK. The Council of Ministers must consult it over certain issues such as agriculture, transport and social policy but is free to consult it on other issues too, should it wish. It acts as a channel of communication from EU institutions to pressure groups.

POLICY-MAKING IN THE EU

The actual policy-making process within the European Union is complex. All new policies or programmes are formally prepared by the Commission. The Commission is often described as the EU's executive branch, because it monitors the implementation of laws adopted by the Council of Ministers. However, it is far from being an apolitical bureaucracy because it has the exclusive right to propose legislation. It is the guardian of the treaties, and as such has to take governments to court; eg, in the 1980s it sued Greece for discriminating against foreign hotel managers, and sued Britain over training requirements for vets. It is therefore the Commission which is the focus of much lobbying by pressure groups, and in particular the 23 directorates-general, each with control over a particular policy area.

After consultation with the Parliament, the ECSC and where appropriate the Committee of the Regions, the Council of Ministers decides on the legislation. *Regulations* do not require legislation, but *directives* always need secondary legislation on the part of national governments. The SEA changed the way in which pressure groups lobby Europe. Prior to its passage, unanimity among member countries was required, therefore pressure groups needed to lobby national governments. With Qualified Majority Voting (QMV) and an increase in power for the European Parliament, groups have changed their tactics, to lobbying the European institutions.

The implications of this shift in power became apparent during the row over the Working Time Directive in 1997, when the European Court of Justice overruled the British government. The government had argued that the opt-out on the Social Chapter meant that the directive did not apply to the UK, but the Commission claimed that it was a matter of health and safety (governed by QMV), and *not* of social policy. The then Prime Minister, John Major actually threatened to wreck the Inter-Governmental Conference over the issue.

ENVIRONMENTAL ISSUES

The drive to create a *single* market widened the Commission's powers over environmental issues, so that policy is harmonised (eg, all pollution controls). The environment is one area where it is obvious that action at nation state level only is inadequate; after all, acid rain and other pollutants do not recognise national frontiers. Prior to the passage of the SEA, the environment was only regulated as part of the attempts to create a *common* market. On most environmental issues, the Council proceeds through QMV, and the Parliament has a role through the 'cooperation procedure'.

The Maastricht Treaty extended the powers of the Parliament over environmental issues. The EU sets standards on water, both for drinking and for swimming in. The British government has been found inadequate in regard to the pollution standards of her beaches just as it has in regard to certain construction projects. The first attempt at privatisation of water had to be abandoned in the face of pressure from the Commission. It was only when the British governments set up the National Rivers Authority that privatisation went ahead.

The EU also regulates air pollution and disposal of waste. By 1990 there was agreement to establish a European Environmental Agency, and in its Environment Programmes, the EU takes great notice of the concept of 'sustainable development'.

Environmental pressure groups such as Greenpeace operate on an international basis, as was seen in their lobbying of the oil company, Shell in the early 1990s, over the disposal of the oil platform Brent Spa in the North Sea. There they mobilised the power of the consumer over both a transnational corporation and the British government under John Major, which was trying to persuade Shell not to surrender to Greenpeace. The company abandoned their plans following a boycott of Shell oil by customers. Because of the presence of Green parties in other European legislatures and in the European Parliament itself, it may well be that environmental groups find the European Union to be a more sympathetic audience than the British government.

THE TRADE UNIONS AND THE SOCIAL CHAPTER

Business groups long ago realised the importance of lobbying Brussels. The trade unions have only recently caught up, and are now establishing offices in Brussels. Just like the political wing of the labour movement (the Labour Party), the British Trade Union movement has traditionally opposed European integration, seeing it as a 'capitalist club'. By 1980 the leftwing part of the Labour Party was pushing an anti-European policy, but it was the block vote of the *unions* which actually enabled that policy to be passed through Conference.

In the wake of the 1987 election defeat, Party leader Neil Kinnock set up the Policy Review to look again at Labour's commitments. One of the issues considered was Europe. The trade unions were now moving in the same direction as the Labour leadership; indeed, Kinnock was only able to get his way within the Labour Party because he carried with him the leaders of the biggest trade unions. It could even be argued that the unions carried the Labour leadership with *them*, that they were the force for change. They had been frozen out of influence by the (Tory) government since 1979, and now saw the European Community as a possible vehicle for influence at a time when Thatcherism was at its strongest.

As the Prime Minister, Margaret Thatcher, became more and more openly hostile to further European integration, the Labour Party and the trade unions became more enthusiastic, with the TUC welcoming 'Frere Jacques' Delors, as the architect of the Social Chapter which aimed at giving rights to workers. As Delors put it, 'one does not fall in love with a single market'; the market had to be made more attractive to ordinary Europeans. Delors told the 1988 Trades Union Congress,

---

'1992 is much more than the creation of an internal market – your movement has a major role to play. Europe needs you.'

The Social Chapter was a product of the late 1980s when unemployment was not the major problem it was to become in the 1990s.

In December 1989 the European Council (heads of government and state within the Union) agreed to sign up for a Community Charter for Workers. The aims of the Social Charter were 'the promotion of employment, improved living and working conditions, proper social protection and dialogue between management and labour'. Only British workers did not have a statutory right to annual leave, or trade union representation. The British government refused to sign, claiming that it was a 'Socialist Charter' which would let in 'socialism by the back door'. The Institute of Directors and to a lesser extent the Confederation of British Industry opposed the Charter. At that stage the Charter had no legal status.

The Conservative governments of the 1980s had reduced the power of the unions; those of the 1990s claimed that this was why the UK had more flexible labour markets, and was therefore benefiting from such huge inward investment from countries such as Japan and South Korea. At the time of the Maastricht Treaty, John Major was willing to consider EMU, but his reaction to the social dimension to a single market was 'no, no, no'. At the German Chancellor, Helmut Kohl's suggestion, the Social Chapter was removed from the Treaty. The other 11 states would go ahead with it, but outside the Treaty. 'Game, set and match to Britain' was Major's claim, and certainly the rest of the Community did not relish a single market where one partner had a competitive advantage in the labour market. For the first time in the history of the Community, a state had been allowed not to accept EEC policies in their totality.

The Labour Party and the unions always argued that the UK should sign the Social Chapter, to give British workers the same rights as those enjoyed in the rest of the EU. During the 1997 election campaign, the TUC ran an advertising campaign arguing that 'elsewhere in Europe employees have basic rights at work, guaranteed by the Social Chapter. Yet the government says the Chapter would reduce our ability to compete and cost 500,000 jobs'. The President of the Commission Jacques Santer accused the British of recreating 'Dickensian sweatshops'.

Within two days of taking office the new Foreign Secretary, Labour's Robin Cook made it clear that the government would sign up to the Social Chapter. The business community, led by the CBI, was relatively relaxed about this, as very little had yet been produced by the Chapter. By 1997, it had produced just two directives, one on works councils and the other on parental leave. When the French car maker Renault closed its Belgian plant in spring 1997 without consulting the workforce, EC President Jacques Santer criticised Renault for breaching the Chapter, but nothing was done. It can be argued that globalisation is a far stronger force than any Social Chapter; if transnational corporations wish to relocate their business, they will undoubtedly do so. Even so, the symbolism of Labour signing up for the Chapter was important.

PRESSURE GROUPS AND EMU

Signing up for the Social Chapter was seen as evidence of a more Euroenthusiastic approach, yet on the really big issues such as EMU, Labour is very cautious. It is not just the British politicians who are ambivalent about European integration. British pressure groups are equally divided. Within the business community for example, the CBI (which represents manufacturing industry) favours EMU, whereas the Institute of Directors (which is more Thatcherite) opposes it. Multinational companies such as British Petroleum (BP) are more enthusiastic than smaller companies. Equally, the TUC General Council currently led by John Monks is in favour of early entry into EMU, whereas many of the more traditional, 'old Labour' union leaders are opposed. They argue that it will necessitate deflationary measures imposed by an unelected central bank, and policies leading to higher unemployment.

The TUC supported British membership of the EMU because, as John Monks told the Lords inquiry into EMU, 'it could be very cold outside a single currency'. By November 1996, the TUC was openly campaigning for UK involvement from the start of EMU in 1999. The same was true of most of the business community, particularly multinationals such as BP headed by David Simon (now Lord Simon, a member of the Blair government), and British Aerospace, whose Chairman attacked John Major in 1996 for failing to restrain the Eurosceptics. This tied in with the warning in February 1997 by Toyota that they might not invest further in Britain if it did not join EMU.

FARMING AND FISHING

Farmers have a significant degree of influence in most political systems. The United States, the home of free enterprise, has subsidised farming since the New Deal of the 1930s. The common market came into existence in 1957, but it was not until the early 1960s under French pressure that a Common Agricultural Policy (CAP) was introduced. In crude terms, this balanced the needs of French farmers against those of German industrialists. The CAP means that when market prices are too low, the European Commission buys farm produce at a higher price. To discourage overproduction, the Commission sometimes pays farmers to take some of their land out of production.

Much of the British hostility towards the EU has centred on the CAP, which has been seen as a grossly expensive way of propping up inefficient French farmers, putting up the price of food for the British consumer, and causing the creation of butter mountains and wine lakes. Because farmers are guaranteed to be able to sell their output, they are *encouraged* to overproduce. This drives prices down and means that the Commission has to spend billions buying up the surplus. Critics argue that the CAP costs the average British household £28 per week. This situation will worsen if the Union expands eastwards, so critics argue that the CAP has to be reformed to cope with enlargement. In her Bruges speech to the College of Europe in September 1988, Margaret Thatcher attacked the wastefulness of the CAP. By 1992, the Community was spending £90 million per annum simply on the destruction of surplus apples. Critics of the EU would argue that it was problems with the EU, in particular over the CAP, which held up the completion of the Uruguay Round of GATT Talks. At one point the then American President, George Bush, threatened to withdraw US troops from Europe if the EC did not cooperate over the talks. Only when reforms of the CAP were agreed in 1992, with the ideas of the agriculture commissioner Ray McSharry, was progress made. The Uruguay Round began in late 1986 but was not finally concluded until 1994. Reform of the CAP thus began in 1992, but even so, it was going to take a lot more change to prepare the CAP for the entry of states such as Poland.

Similar hostility is directed at the Common Fisheries Policy (CFP) which is portrayed as responsible for the plight of British trawlermen. The CFP governs access to EU waters and quotas. Another controversial policy aims at conserving stocks of fish by allocating quotas to each member state; however, there have been problems over 'quota hopping' – ie, netting more fish than the quota allows. Spanish 'quota hopping' lay behind the passage of the Merchant Shipping Act of 1988, which prevented non-British citizens from registering boats as British in order to be able to qualify for the UK's fish quota. In the Factortame case, the European Court of Justice overturned the British law lords' refusal to grant an injunction to Spanish fishing companies against the British government. By

March 1996, the Spanish fishermen were suing the British government for compensation, for the time that they were prevented from fishing in the UK.

British farmers have benefited from CAP, although arguably British agriculture has long been more efficient than farming in other EU countries. The repeal of the Corn Laws in 1846 forced British agriculture to compete with foreign products, and even by the beginning of the twentieth century, the percentage of the British workforce engaged in agriculture was tiny in comparison with that of France, Italy or Germany. The British peasantry died out long, long ago, so there is no social equivalent of the French or Greek peasant class. British farms tend to be relatively large and capital intensive in comparison with their European counterparts.

British farmers have always enjoyed close working relations with British governments of every party, and the Agriculture Act 1947 actually obliges the government to consult farm pressure groups. The National Farmers Union (NFU) is one of the most powerful pressure groups of all, so much so that the Ministry of Agriculture Fisheries and Food has been regarded as the 'sponsoring' ministry for the NFU. During the salmonella crisis of 1988 the NFU managed to get the then Health Minister Edwina Currie dismissed for her derogatory comments about British egg production. Yet, eight years later in the crisis over BSE, consumer concerns and the power of the European Commission revealed the relative powerlessness of the farmers and of their pressure group.

THE BSE CRISIS

The BSE affair of 1996 focused Tory discontent over things European, just when the Intergovernmental Conference was supposedly addressing the difficult issues posed by enlargement. Five days after the Health Secretary had announced a suspected link between bovine spongiform encephalitis (BSE) in cows and Creuzfeldt-Jacob disease (CJD) in humans, the European Commission announced a global ban on British beef products. The British Agriculture Minister, Douglas Hogg, proposed a partial cull, but the Commission wanted more, and refused to compensate Britain financially on the scale the British were demanding. Sales of all beef in Europe collapsed and Europe's beef farmers were up in arms. The irony was that Europe's farmers had always been the clearest beneficiaries of the Community.

The British government reacted by arguing that it was the EU ban that had caused the collapse of confidence in British beef. This was music to the ears of Eurosceptics like Tory MP Teddy Taylor, who claimed that Britain's European partners 'seem to do everything they can to humiliate Britain'. John Major described it as the biggest crisis facing Britain since the Falklands war. There was even talk of a 'beef election' in which the Tories would present themselves as patriots against the pro-European Labour/Liberal forces. The Tory election campaign poster of spring 1997 showed a tearful British lion with the slogan 'New Labour, new Eurodanger', but opinion polls in Britain showed that a 2:1 majority blamed the government, not the Europeans, over the BSE crisis.

The British government claimed the EU ban was illegal under Article 173 of the Treaty of Rome, but in fact the ban was global; it was not confined to the European Union, and there was never talk of retaliation against the USA, Australia, Canada or New Zealand, or non-cooperation in NATO or the Commonwealth. By May 21st 1996, John Major had instituted a policy of non-cooperation in the EU, reminiscent of Charles De Gaulle's 'empty chair policy' of 1965 or Margaret Thatcher's obstruction over the budget in 1984. Even the Cabinet's staunchest pro-Europeans, Kenneth Clarke and Michael Heseltine went along with Major's policy. Two Ministers, Lady Chalker and Roger Freeman, neither of them sceptics, blocked European business. By June 1st Britain had imposed over 20 vetoes; 77 Community actions were to be blocked over 23 days. Of course many of these issues were trivial, but even so, the ban gave an indication of the sheer volume of Community business, and therefore how important membership had become to British politics.

SUMMARY

Pressure groups are involved in lobbying those with power. It is no coincidence that many British pressure groups were alert to the potential importance of the European Community long before the issue began to dominate the domestical political agenda. Whether it be groups seeking to use the European Union to pursue a positive agenda (as in the Trade Unions seeking British implementation of the Social Chapter), or groups trying to block developments in Europe (as in the farmers trying to overturn decisions about BSE), it is clear that pressure groups cannot afford to ignore the EU if they are to achieve their objectives.

STUDY GUIDES

Your notes must make clear exactly what a pressure group is, and how it differs from a political party. You also need to be clear as to the ways in which the organisation of the European Union affects the way in which pressure groups operate. Try to separate the different ways in which Europe has affected such groups as the farmers and the unions, environmental groups and business.

Exam Hints

1 *'More and more decisions are made in Brussels rather than at Westminster or in Whitehall, therefore pressure groups direct their attentions there'. Discuss.*

2 *How does the debate over the Social Chapter reveal the importance of the European Union to the British trade unions?*

Both essays require you to examine the details of the policy-making process; away from the headlines, pressure groups get on with the practical business of attempting to make policy serve their interests. You need to illustrate this through examples, either lots of examples but not in great detail, or one or two reasonably detailed case studies. Either way, you must contrast the decision-making processes within the nation state, with those of this intergovernmental organisation. Within the UK, the standard description of pressure group influence has been that insider groups get their way by lobbying the Executive, in particular civil servants, but the EU is a much more complex structure. It may well be that in order to be successful, groups have to 'work on' different institutions at the same time: the Commission, the bureaucrats working for the Council of Ministers (known as COREPER), the European Parliament, perhaps even the judges of the ECJ.

The relationship between the British trade unions and the EU is an interesting case in point. Here is a movement that was traditionally hostile to the Community, which then changed its mind. Your essay needs to consider all the factors behind this change – internal and external, practical and ideological. The actual details of the Social Chapter are not what matters; what is important is what this issue reveals about the nature of politics in an increasingly interdependent world. The Chapter was an attempt at establishing uniform rights, but one state 'opted out'. The sequel is, of course, that the UK *did* sign under the new Labour government, but a precedent had been set which other states and other groups will take note of. Your essay again needs to be analytical rather than descriptive.

Practice Questions

1 Why, and with what consequences, have British pressure groups spent more time and resources lobbying Europe?

2 What are the main access points available to pressure groups wishing to lobby Europe?

7

THE IMPACT OF EUROPE ON BRITISH FOREIGN AND DEFENCE POLICY

Introduction

THIS CHAPTER CONSIDERS the areas covered by the second pillar of the Maastricht Treaty, foreign and defence policy. The EU is by far the world's biggest donor of aid to other countries, and its military forces include two nuclear powers, Britain and France. It could be argued that membership of this body offers Britain a chance to exercise diplomatic leverage in a world dominated by large states and blocs. Those who favoured British entry into the Community in the early days argued that in exchange for a limited loss of sovereignty, the UK would become part of a major force in which there is a pooling of sovereignty. However, it is one thing to devise common policies on agriculture, fisheries, or even monetary union; it is quite another altogether to agree foreign and defence policies. These take us to the very heart of what sovereignty means, and no state gives up control of these issues lightly. Some British people are perhaps especially wary over co-ordinating foreign and defence policies, because they believe that British history is a record of independence.

Key Points
This chapter contains material on the following key issues:

- Britain's relationship with the United States.
- Britain's relationship with her European neighbours.
- The impact of the Bosnian War upon the European Union.

A BACKGROUND TO BRITISH POLICY

The UK has not been occupied by a foreign power since the Norman Conquest of 1066. It was the existence of the 22 mile stretch of water known as the English Channel, which prevented Spain conquering England in the sixteenth century, Napoleon in the nineteenth and Hitler in the twentieth. So ingrained is this notion of Britain apart, that some people opposed the construction of the Channel Tunnel on the grounds that it would end a physical separation that had served Britain well. If there was a natural British sympathy, it was with the 'kith and kin' of the Commonwealth, the settlers who had gone from Britain to Australia, Canada, New Zealand, Rhodesia (now Zimbabwe) and South Africa in the last century, or with fellow English speakers in the USA. There was no natural affinity with our European neighbours.

Twice this century, in 1914 and 1939, Britain had gone to war to prevent German domination of Europe. No one could therefore accuse the UK of being isolationist, but on both occasions it required American assistance to defeat Germany, just as after the Second World War it would require US help to contain the Soviet Union. In the immediate aftermath of the Second World War, it looked as though the Americans might revert to the same kind of isolationist policies they had followed after the First World War; the pro-isolationist Republican Party won control of Congress in the November 1946 elections. It was the British decision to abandon the fight against the Greek Communists in February 1947 that persuaded the Americans that Britain was indeed in dire straits economically, and that the USA would have to take over Britain's role of world policeman, to step in to defend the 'free world' against Communism. In the Truman Doctrine of March 1947, President Truman made this commitment, and three months later the American Secretary of State, George Marshall, offered economic assistance to wartorn Europe.

The British took full part in the Marshall Plan of 1947 which brought American aid into Western Europe, and the Brussels Treaty of 1948 which brought together France, Belgium, Holland, Luxembourg and Britain, to defend themselves against Germany and the USSR. Ernest Bevin, one of the greatest British Foreign Secretaries of the twentieth century, used to say of the Germans 'I tries 'ard but I 'ates em'. However, Bevin also wanted a prosperous Germany, believing that this would prevent political extremism there. By 1948, British pilots who just three years earlier had been bombing Berlin, helped to supply West Berlin by air to prevent it from succumbing to Stalin. In no sense could the UK be regarded as turning her back on Europe.

Most British PMs have appeared more interested in the so-called 'special relationship' with the USA, than in Britain's European role. This Atlanticist approach was especially true of Margaret Thatcher. Her admiration for the USA in general and Ronald Reagan's administration (1981–89) in particular was fully reciprocated, which perhaps encouraged her in the view that Europe was simply a free trade zone, whereas Britain's political and security interests lay with the USA.

THE FORMATION OF NATO

The main British objective following the Second World War was to tie the USA into the defence of Western Europe against Soviet Communism, an objective achieved with the creation of the North Atlantic Treaty Organisation (NATO) in 1949. Britain's former Ambassador to the USA, Nicholas Henderson argues that 'no other abdication of sovereignty as great as this has occurred in British history', and yet British membership of NATO has never proved to be a contentious issue. It could be because NATO is an alliance system in which members states delegate authority upwards, but ultimately remain sovereign; eg, France left full membership of NATO in the 1960s; NATO could also simply reflect the Atlanticist leanings of the British.

Even when the Labour left was at the peak of its power in the early 1980s and had persuaded the party to adopt a unilateralist position, it never promoted an anti-NATO stance. Some on the left of the Labour Party, like Chris Mullin and Brian Sedgemore, converted to the European issue in the 1980s as a way of reducing British dependence on the USA. In Mullin's eyes,

---

'a common foreign and defence policy would release this country from its slavish dependence on the US which has been the shameful hallmark of all postwar British foreign policy.'

The New Statesman

However, such an anti-American position was a minority one. It is not just the British political leaders who have been Atlanticist since the war; most British people feel the same. Yet in one of the many ironies of this whole situation, the Americans have long tried to persuade the British to be more integrationist in Europe. It was an American President, J.F. Kennedy, who helped persuade the British government to apply for membership in 1961.

THE EUROPEAN DEFENCE COMMUNITY

The fact that Europeans wanted British involvement in integration can be seen from the 1952 French proposals to create a European Defence Community (EDC), which would include Britain and their mutual former enemy, West Germany. The Korean War had begun in 1950, with US-led forces fighting Communist North Korea. The Americans wanted the Europeans to incorporate West German forces into their anti-Soviet defences. The Conservatives under Winston Churchill were back in power, and the Foreign Secretary Anthony Eden made it clear that Britain would not join an EDC. In the event, the French Assembly killed off the plan in 1954.

The alternative was the British proposal, the Western European Union (WEU), which in 1955 built on the Brussels Treaty by incorporating Italy and West Germany. The WEU still exists, indeed it was given an expanded role by the Maastricht Treaty, but there are serious problems integrating it into the EU.

EUROPEAN POLITICAL COOPERATION

European political cooperation dates back to the Davignon Report of 1970, which created a pattern of regular meetings of foreign ministers to produce a joint foreign policy. At first the procedures were voluntary and because it was outside the EC treaties, implementation proved difficult. There was no real consensus over the problems of the Middle East in the 1970s, or over the Falklands crisis in 1982.

Despite American urgings, the British governments were always wary of integrating defence and foreign policy with Europe. They saw the UK as a global power, with a permanent seat on the Security Council of the United Nations and a nuclear arsenal of her own. Admittedly the UK was no longer as great a power as she once had been, but episodes such as the Falklands War showed she still had strength; indeed, Margaret Thatcher argued that it put the 'great' back into Great Britain.

The Falklands War of 1982, in which the British had (with American help) retaken the Falklands Islands from the Argentineans with very low casualties on the British side, convinced Margaret Thatcher that British nationalism was a potent force. Speaking after the British victory, Thatcher claimed,

> *'We have ceased to be a nation in retreat. We have a new confidence, born in the economic battles at home, tested and found true 8,000 miles way. We rejoice that Britain has rekindled the spirit which fired her for generations past and which has begun to burn as brightly as before.'*

There was much muttering within both the Tory Party and the British press over the 'failure' of the European Community to back Britain on the Falklands issue, in contrast to the help given by the Reagan Administration in the USA. This was partly a product of the difficulties the Community faced, given that by 1982, Spain (who has special ties with South America) was moving towards membership; but this attitude simply encouraged the Atlanticist in Margaret Thatcher. As Michael Clarke puts it, Thatcher was a 'radical Conservative in domestic policy but a very conservative Conservative in foreign policy'.

As far back as 1973, the then US Secretary of State, Henry Kissinger was bemoaning the fact that no one person 'spoke for Europe'. The Single European Act of 1986 was supposed to improve Community action over foreign and security policy by putting it on a legal basis and creating a secretariat for European political cooperation. However, there was no question of enforcing a common approach. It was the ending of the Cold War in the late 1980s that put the issue of European political cooperation high up the agenda.

The Eurosceptics in Britain used Community inaction over the Gulf War in 1991 (only Britain, France and Italy took part) to draw the triumphant conclusion that there could be no real European foreign policy and defence policy. In a memorable debate in the Commons, just before John Major and Douglas Hurd went to Maastricht to negotiate the Treaty of European Union, Margaret Thatcher, Edward Heath and Dennis Healey (former Labour Chancellor) all spoke, the latter warning that the belief that federalism would solve the problem of nationalism 'flies in the face not only of history but of recent experience'. The Soviet coup of August 1991 (Communist hard-liners had tried to overthrow the President of the USSR, Mikhail Gorbachev, and instead strengthened Boris Yeltsin, the President of Russia) and the subsequent disintegration of the USSR seemed to confirm Healey's view (speaking in the House of Commons) that,

---

'the most important issue we face today is that of enlarging the community ... [It is] the best and only hope for the east European countries to make the transition to stable democracies and prosperous market economies ... If they fail to make that transition the consequences for western Europe could be cataclysmic ... Widening the community must take precedence, if necessary, over deepening it.'

A COMMON FOREIGN AND SECURITY POLICY

The Maastricht Treaty created a Common Foreign and Security Policy (CFSP) as the second pillar of the European Union, with WEU as the defence component. The Parliament and the Commission have a very limited role to play in the process. At the time of the Maastricht Treaty, the leaders considered and then rejected the idea of creating a single voice on foreign policy. Decisions on *whether* to act require unanimity from the Council of Ministers, but decisions on *how* to act can be taken by QMV.

The British were wary of empowering the WEU, because it might undermine NATO. Their wish was to put the WEU under NATO. One problem is that the WEU itself has no troops, although parts of the national armies of member states are formally answerable to it. The French and the Germans wanted the WEU to be integrated into the EU, but both the British government and the states which were neutral during the Cold War (Sweden, Ireland, Austria and Finland) oppose this.

The Albanian affair of March 1997, when a European state appeared to be on the verge of falling apart and there were demands for EU intervention, exposed the limitations of European political cooperation. Because it is an intergovernmental process, action requires unanimity which is difficult to achieve, and the CFSP did nothing to prevent war in the former Yugoslavia.

THE CRISIS OVER YUGOSLAVIA

Yugoslavia, a multi-ethnic, multi-religious country of about 23 million people, was a federal state made up of six republics. It was dominated by Serbia, which contained 40 per cent of the population and contained the nation's capital, Belgrade. There had been tensions within the state from the death of Tito (the head of state in Yugoslavia 1945–80) from 1980 onwards. The collapse of the Soviet satellite states in 1989 provoked further conflict in Yugoslavia. A series of clashes began in Kosovo, a part of southern Serbia which previously enjoyed a degree of self government. Serbia's President Milosevic imposed direct rule in 1989, despite the fact that the majority of the population was of Albanian origin. By May 1991 there was the threat of civil war between two republics Serbia and Croatia, as Serbia blocked the installation of a Croat as head of the collective presidency. Croatia voted for independence in June 1991. Serb minorities in Croatia and Bosnia wanted the protection of the federal army dominated by the Serbs; war broke out between Serbia and Croatia.

Luxembourg's Foreign Minister, Jacques Poos, proclaimed 'this is the hour of Europe, not America' when he headed for Yugoslavia in June 1991 as the EU spokesman. Together with a representative from Portugal and Holland he brokered a ceasefire, but it had broken down by July. The EC imposed an arms embargo on all Yugoslav Republics in September 1991, and the former Tory Foreign Secretary (and at that stage General Secretary of NATO) Lord Carrington chaired a peace conference; this proposed a confederation, a plan rejected by Serbia. Cruise O'Brien blames Germany for initiating the Yugoslav crisis by recognising Croatia and Slovenia as sovereign states in December 1991. The rest of the Community followed suit in January 1992. By January 1992 as a result of the Serbia–Croatia war, 10,000 people had died and Croatia had lost one-third of its territory.

Bosnia and Herzgovinia followed Croatia's lead and left the Yugoslav federation in 1991. By April 1992, the international community recognised the Bosnian government as a sovereign state, and the Bosnian war began as Serb minorities claimed that they were being denied rights. European governments had recognised Bosnia but were not willing to give the help necessary to protect it. The UK took over the EC Presidency in July 1992 by which time the genocide in Bosnia had begun ('ethnic cleansing' was the principle used to justify the killing of the large Muslim population). However, the British did not use the Presidency to attempt to end the war but instead blocked any such initiatives, particularly from France and Holland. John Major did host a EC–UN conference in London on the fate of the former Yugoslavia. The UN sent peacekeeping forces to Croatia and Bosnia, and the EU and the UN sent mediators – the former British Foreign Secretary David Owen who had held office in James Callaghan's Labour government, and the former US Secretary of State, Cyrus Vance who had served Democrat President, Jimmy Carter. Their proposals, known as the Owen–Vance plan, attempted to preserve a multi-ethnic Bosnia, but it was backed neither by Washington nor by the European states, and had clearly failed by 1993. The UN set up 'safe havens' for Muslims, but even this was ignored when in July 1995 thousands of Muslims were massacred in the supposed safe haven of Srebrenica. It was this which finally provoked President Clinton into action. Four years after Poos's statement, nothing had been achieved, and it was the American influence which negotiated a peace for Bosnia with the Dayton Accords of November 1995. This effectively returned to the Carrington plan, dividing Bosnia along ethnic lines.

The European failure to deal with Yugoslavia, a European problem, exposed the pretensions of European political cooperation. Many critics blame the European dithering over Bosnia between 1991 and 1995 on Britain in particular. In a sense, the Foreign Secretary, Douglas Hurd, was following traditional British foreign policy, which has never seen Eastern Europe as a vital sphere of interest to the British, unlike Western Europe. European inactivity over the Balkans was not the sole or even the main cause of the crisis, but it did illustrate the difficulties of producing a coherent foreign policy.

BRITAIN, FRANCE AND GERMANY — THE ETERNAL TRIANGLE

By the time of the Intergovernmental Conference in 1997, France and Germany wanted some extension of QMV over foreign policy and, something which is anathema to Britain and the neutrals, eventual merging of the WEU into the EU. The Franco–German relationship has been at the heart of the European project from the beginning, and in a sense the British have long played the outsider in this eternal triangle of powers.

Two weeks after rejecting the British application to join the EC in January 1963, President De Gaulle signed the Franco–German Treaty. A close Franco–German relationship was to be the basis of the Community thereafter. Yet there have been obvious tensions between France and Germany. One of the reasons why the French attitude towards British membership of the Community changed in 1969, was that France wanted a counterweight to the increasingly dominant economic power of West Germany; it was hoped that Britain would provide one.

For a brief period in the early 1970s under Edward Heath, Britain did manage to turn the Franco–German nucleus of the Community into a triangular relationship including the UK. Yet from Edward Heath's removal in 1974, Britain appeared to revert to a more obstructionist approach. This was true of Harold Wilson and James Callaghan, but especially of Margaret Thatcher.

THE REUNIFICATION OF GERMANY

In the autumn of 1989, the Communist regimes of Eastern Europe were falling one by one. Mikhail Gorbachev made it plain that the USSR would not intervene to prevent this process in the way that former USSR President Nikita Khrushchev had crushed the dissident Hungarians in 1956, or Leonid Brezhnev had sent the tanks into Czechoslovakia in 1968. The order within which Europe had lived since the Marshall Plan (1947) was visibly disintegrating.

In November 1989, the Berlin Wall came down, and the reunification of Germany re-emerged as a diplomatic issue. The sudden collapse of East Germany prompted President Mitterand to conclude an agreement with Chancellor Helmut Kohl at the Strasbourg summit in the Autumn of 1989; an agreement which put Franco–German weight behind the Delors Report (the report advocating EMU).

The formal reunification of Germany in October 1990 meant that, with a population of over 80 million, Germany was now by far the largest member state rather than simply one of the big four. The balance which had existed since the creation of the Community (France and Germany of roughly equal size, flanked by Italy and later on Britain) had gone. Margaret Thatcher opposed reunification on the grounds that Germany would be too strong. She summoned British historians of Germany to Downing Street in March 1990, to discuss the 'German problem'; she told them that there was something distinctly expansionist in the German national psyche. On one occasion she said that it would be 'at least another 40 years before the British could trust the Germans again'.

By the summer of 1990, one of her closest colleagues in Cabinet, the Secretary of State for the Environment Nicholas Ridley, was saying much the same thing, but in more colourful language, to the editor of *The Spectator*, Dominic Lawson. Ridley argued that the Kohl government and the Bundesbank were creating a Fourth Reich. He condemned EMU as 'a German racket designed to take over the whole of Europe'. He went on to say 'I'm not against giving up sovereignty in principle but not to this lot. You might just as well give it to Hitler'. He was forced to resign, but many assumed he was simply saying publicly what Margaret Thatcher was saying privately.

The French drew a very different conclusion to Margaret Thatcher; they believed that Germany must be bound into the Community ever more tightly to *prevent* German domination of Europe. Kohl agreed with Mitterand, preferring to see a 'European Germany' rather than a 'German Europe'.

MAJOR AND KOHL

Speaking in Germany shortly after his elevation to Prime Minister, John Major promised a new start.

> *'My aims for Britain in the Community can be simply stated. I want us to be where we belong, at the very heart of Europe'.*

Major and his new party chairman Chris Patten advocated a social market economy based on the ideas of the German Christian Democrats. This combines a commitment to a free market economy, with protection for the workforce in the form of guaranteed rights and generous welfare. It contrasts with the so-called Anglo-Saxon capitalism as practised by the USA and by Thatcherite Britain, where there is a move towards a minimal state and as much as possible is left to the marketplace. With Major/Patten in power, the British Conservative MEPs who tend to be more pro-Europe than their Westminster counterparts, were supposed to unite with the German Christian Democrat MEPs.

However, by the spring of 1991 the idea had been dropped. Although the Tory Party had removed Margaret Thatcher, its economic and social policies remained firmly Thatcherite, and that meant a divergence from German conservatism rather than a convergence. By the time that the UK had left the ERM in September 1992, the close relationship Major and Kohl had enjoyed in 1990 had given way to antagonism.

The election of the Gaullist Jacques Chirac as President of France in May 1995 was supposed to help John Major, because he was reputedly less *communitaire* (pro-EU) than his predecessor. At a summit with Major, Chirac proclaimed there could be 'no Europe without Britain'. Chirac had opposed the SEA, reluctantly voted yes to the Maastricht Treaty, and had opposed Portuguese and Spanish membership. Chirac described the Franco–German relationship as 'necessary but not sufficient'. Kohl wanted to strengthen the European Parliament; Chirac wanted to strengthen the Council of Ministers over the Parliament. Yet for all their differences, Chirac established a close relationship with Kohl (who had been re-elected in October 1994), and both made it clear they were determined to go ahead with EMU.

So, while Germany and France were coming together once more, the British appeared to be drifting away. The Defence Secretary Michael Portillo told the 1995 Tory conference 'we will not allow Brussels to control our defence policy'; he stressed that servicemen gave their lives 'for Britain, not for Brussels'.

BLAIR AND KOHL

In the 1997 General Election campaign, Tory posters depicted Tony Blair as a dummy sitting on Kohl's knee. The slogan 'don't send a boy to do a man's job' clearly implied that Blair would be a 'soft touch' on Europe. Pro-European Conservatives such as Leon Brittan and Edward Heath were appalled at such clumsy and dangerous propaganda, but the party leadership believed that Labour were vulnerable over the European issue. In February 1998, John Redwood criticised the decision to honour Helmut Kohl by making him a

Freeman of the City of London. Redwood claimed that Blair had forced the City to do it, although party leader William Hague rebuked Redwood for this.

It is true that the other European leaders were hoping for a change of government in the UK in 1997 (this was one reason for delaying completion of the IGC), and certainly the election of Labour was welcomed. Although the British hesitation over EMU has disappointed Britain's European partners, there are attempts to promote closer relations between Britain and Europe.

In January 1998 the British assumed the Presidency of the European Union and although that was when the key decisions on EMU were to be taken, it was clear that the UK had a limited role to play. In the September 1998 elections in Germany, voters rejected the Conservative Kohl who had been Chancellor for 16 years, longer than anyone since Bismarck. The socialist leader Gerhard Schroeder will lead a coalition government which will aim to establish good relations with the moderate left governments of Britain, Italy and France. Schroeder is in favour of the euro but believes that more needs to be done to bring down German unemployment. Germany and France are determined that the UK will enter EMU, and should not be penalised for delay in doing so. To that end they have 'reserved' a place for Britain on the European Central Bank, but European Finance Ministers are reluctant to allow their British counterpart, Gordon Brown, a role on the key committees planning for EMU, when the UK is staying out for the duration.

By the time of the European summit on unemployment in November 1997, Tony Blair was seen as a key player, honouring his pledge that Britain would be at the centre of Europe, even though the UK was staying out of EMU for the moment. On January 1st 1998 in the ceremony at Waterloo Station, in which Britain assumed the Presidency of the European Union, Blair announced that the theme of the British Presidency would be independence combined with cooperation, a theme embodied in a logo designed by British and European children (shown on the cover of this book). It took the arch-sceptic John Redwood to point out that Waterloo has rather different connotations for the French.

SUMMARY

One of the most sensitive issues for any sovereign state is the extent to which it can surrender control over its foreign and security policies. It is therefore not surprising that the coordination of such policies has proved very problematic for the European Union. This is a problem that is not unique to the UK; the French for example are just as keen on retaining control over their own defence forces, including their nuclear arsenal. However, again it is true that the UK has had particular problems in this area, problems that are linked to the British sense of separateness from Europe. It is not just Conservative governments that have looked instinctively towards the US for leadership; so have Labour governments, and in that sense there is not much that is new about Blair's government.

STUDY GUIDES

As with all other topics dealt with in the book, what is important about your notes is that they convey the way issues developed and changed over time. You are not required to know masses of historical detail, but you *do* need some detail in order to illustrate your arguments. The material dealt with here is different from that on other topics, because it looks at issues through a diplomatic or foreign policy lens. This takes it closer to international relations, but of course that has always been one of the crucial issues involved in the European project. Part of the reason that the UK stayed out of the EC originally was that it felt it had a 'special relationship' with the USA, and your notes need to address the reasons for believing that this was the case, as well as evidence that the 'special relationship' was an illusion.

The most appropriate diagram to consider at this point would be that of Churchill's three circles and the best use to make of it would be to think about how relevant, if at all, the notion of the UK as at the centre of these relationships remains. How much has changed in the last half century?

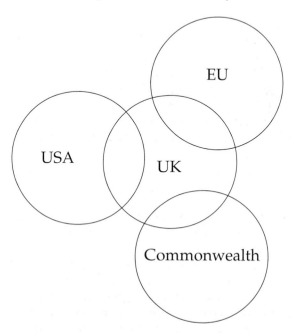

Exam Hints

1   'The "special relationship" which the UK should have promoted was that with Germany and France'. Discuss.

This question invites you to consider the triangular relationship, Germany, France and the UK. This is not to say that other states such as Italy and Spain are not important, simply to reassert that the relationship which has driven the European project forward is that between France and Germany; even now, if the UK is serious about being a leader in Europe, then the British will have to reconsider their attitude towards these two states in particular. This will also require a reassessment of the British relationship with the United States, a relationship that has been the cornerstone of postwar foreign and defence policy, and still is, as events in the Gulf in the early part of 1998 showed (the USA and the UK threatened to bomb Iraq over its failure to comply with UN weapons inspectors). You will be expected to argue both ways, yes the British should have put more emphasis on the European angle, versus no, they should not, and they were right to value the USA more.

2   Is it ever going to be possible to have an effective common foreign and security policy?

This essay provokes a discussion about the feasibility and desirability of ceding sovereignty over an issue as sensitive as foreign and defence policy. Again, try to plan it as a 'yes it is' versus a 'no it is not' essay. Give reasons for thinking that each might be true, and then in the conclusion try to synthesise them; in other words, stress that our answer hinges on what exactly we mean by effective – these terms are ambiguous and not self-explanatory. Illustrate your arguments by contrasting foreign and defence policy with other policies such as agriculture and finance. Why might it be possible to move forward in some policy areas but not others?

Practice Questions

1 Why has it proved so difficult to coordinate foreign and defence policies and what have been the consequences of this failure?
2 'The concerns over national sovereignty mean that there can never be a common foreign and security policy.' How true is this?

8

THE FUTURE OF THE EUROPEAN UNION

Introduction

THIS CHAPTER LOOKS at the future development of the European Union, in particular the vexed question of enlargement. Given that the European project has always been dynamic rather than static, it is impossible to simply freeze the existing form of the Union and make it permanent. The two issues of enlargement (widening the scope of the EU) and Economic and Monetary Union (deepening this scope) are urgent items on the agenda, and are not going to go away.

Key points

This chapter contains material on the following key issues:

- Countries who wish to join the EU, and why this causes difficulties.
- Why deepening European commitment might be seen as an alternative to widening.
- The Treaty of Amsterdam 1997.
- Likely developments within the EU over the next few years.

WIDENING

12 MEMBERS BECOME 15

The December 1994 summit in Essen took place just after the cliff-hanging referendum in Norway, when for the second time the Norwegians voted against entry of the EU. Even without Norway, the EU expanded from 12 member countries to 15 in January 1995 as Finland, Austria and Sweden (all unable to join during the Cold War because they were neutral) came in.

These countries had been members of the European Free Trade Association (EFTA), but unlike Norway and Switzerland, had decided to go for full membership of the EU. There was always support within the British Tory party for enlargement, particularly the bringing in of all wealthy countries which would be net contributors to the budget. However, dilution of the veto was an entirely different matter, a question of politics not economics. John Major insisted in 1994 that enlargement should not lead to a change in the number of votes (23) needed to block a proposal at the Council of Ministers. He argued that it was necessary on grounds of fairness, as the power of the large countries should not be further whittled down by small ones. Every EU institution is biased in favour of countries with small populations. The five largest states, Germany, France, the UK, Italy and Spain account for 80 per cent of the population of the EU, and have just over half the votes. In fact in the end, Major backed down and accepted an increase to 26 votes. This was called the **Ionnina Compromise** (it was agreed at Ionnina at Corfu).

15 MEMBERS BECOME 26?

There is a list of potential applicants to join the EU, at the head of which are Malta and Cyprus. Germany is anxious to incorporate Poland, Hungary, the former Czechoslovakia and Slovenia. Known collectively as the Visegrad states, they are all traditional German spheres of influence. John Major agreed but wanted to go further, broadening the EU to include not only the Scandinavian countries and the former Communist states of Eastern Europe, but also perhaps Russia. Helmut Kohl believes that tightening (ie, further integration) is the essential prerequisite for enlargement; Major believed the opposite – widening as an alternative to deepening.

Either way, widening poses an enormous cost. To integrate the Visegrad four states alone would mean an increase of 60 per cent of the existing budget. Of the 15 existing members, four are classed as poor, and therefore entitled to substantial transfers. If the 11 ex-Communist states were to join, the number would rise to 15 out of 26. An IGC began at Turin in March 1996 (just as the BSE scare broke out) and lasted until June 1997. The crucial issue was enlargement to prevent instability in Eastern Europe. Enlargement had implications for the CAP and for the institutional rules of the EU. Of the 11 potential applicants, only Poland has a big population, so there are demands for a change to voting weights. On existing weightings Germany, Britain and Holland with 42 per cent of the Union's population cannot block a proposal, while Greece, Belgium, Portugal, Denmark, Finland, Ireland and Luxembourg with 12 per cent of the population, can do so. Because each country retains at least one commissioner, if further enlargement proceeds the Commission would swell to around 40 people.

DEEPENING

On the 40th anniversary of the Treaty of Rome in March 1997, the Dutch government built upon the draft Irish Treaty of December 1995. They added clauses on home affairs, a common foreign policy and 'flexibility'. The then Foreign Secretary, Malcolm Rifkind objected, on the ground that the Dutch were trying to reopen the Maastricht Treaty debate by making the second and third pillars (foreign policy and home affairs) supranational. Again, the notion that some states could integrate faster than others, was raised as a way of avoiding conflict within the Union. The most difficult issue remained EMU.

THE AMSTERDAM TREATY

By the time the IGC ended in late June 1997, the Labour Party was in power in Britain. Most of the European leaders saw the change of government in Britain as a positive step, believing that it would lead to a more integrationist approach. European socialists such as the former French minister Elizabeth Guigou wanted the IGC to end the national veto, give more powers to the European Parliament and extend QMV to virtually every aspect of EU policy including policing, immigration, foreign affairs and defence. However, the British Labour Party was very wary of anything which smacked of federalism. It wanted majority voting extended to cover social affairs, the environment and industrial policy, but not home affairs, taxation or security. The Labour Foreign Secretary Robin Cook stated Labour's approach:

> *'first Britain must sign up to the social dimension of Europe ... secondly there must be a fundamental reform of the CAP ... thirdly Labour will put jobs back at the top of the priorities of Europe'.*

Labour want a European Commission which is more accountable to the European Parliament, and a Council of Ministers more accountable to national parliaments.

The intergovernmental conference of 1996–97 was supposed to address the problem of enlargement of other institutional problems, but largely failed to do so. Despite the apocalyptic warnings of people such as Michael Howard (who claimed that the IGC may produce a treaty that meant the end of the United Kingdom as a nation state), the Amsterdam Treaty was largely a tidying-up measure, not remotely comparable to the Maastricht Treaty or the Single European Act in its importance. At the Summit, enlargement was discussed, but a Treaty was agreed which avoided the most difficult issues. However, at some point in the not too distant future, European politicians including the British will have to address serious issues concerning the future direction of the European project. Enlargement and EMU are simply the two biggest issues facing the Union; there are plenty of others, from border control to relations with the rest of the world.

TONY BLAIR AT THE AMSTERDAM SUMMIT, JUNE 1997

THE FUTURE?

It is possible that Economic and Monetary Union will fail, and that this will lead to a collapse of the European Union itself. Some sceptics positively welcomed the arrival of EMU for precisely this reason, believing that the EU had seriously overreached itself and that the public backlash against the collapse of EMU would be even greater than the disillusionment caused by the 'failure' of the Exchange Rate Mechanism in 1992–93. However, examination of European integration since 1945 shows that while there are occasional retreats (such as failure over EDC in 1954, the initial rejection of British applications to join the EC, the stalemate over De Gaulle's empty chair policy in the 1960s, the 'Eurosclerosis' of the late 1970s), there are also periods of advance, when the problems holding the project back appear to be overcome and the structure takes an almost quantum leap forward. For example:

- the creation of the ECSC in 1950
- the signing of the Treaty of Rome in 1957
- the Hague Summit of 1969 leading to the first enlargement in 1973
- the Single European Act of 1986
- the Treaty of European Union of 1991 at Maastricht
- the creation of EMU in 1999

were moments when the federalist dream of 'ever closer union' came closer to fruition.

The likelihood is therefore that even if EMU does fail, it will not mean an end to attempts at European integration. The political elites of most European states have simply invested too much in European integration to wash their hands of it now, after almost half a century. If anything, the opposite is true; the elites will have to generate a greater degree of public support for integration. The rest of the world is not standing still. The signing of the North American Free Trade Agreement (1993) in the first Clinton term and its possible extension to the rest of the Americas in the years to come, as well as similar developments in Asia, mean that the world is increasingly divided into regional blocs. The Unionist MP Joe Chamberlain was warning at the beginning of the twentieth century 'the days of small nations are over, the days of great empire are upon us'. The comment looks even more apt at the end of the century.

Integration will probably continue, and it will be accompanied by difficult choices about a whole range of policy matters. Wish as they might, British politicians cannot avoid answering questions about these pressing issues. It is not that the Labour Party is any more able to resist these pressures than the Conservatives. From the very beginning, the European issue has divided both major British parties and will doubtless continue to do so. It is clear that Europe is going to remain an enormously complex and contentious aspect of British politics for the foreseeable future.

SUMMARY

It is always difficult and to some extent unwise to speculate about the future. Very few people would have foreseen in April 1992, when John Major won re-election, that within a few months the pound would be driven off the ERM and the Treaty of European Union would be in jeopardy. As Mrs Thatcher said, 'in politics always expect the unexpected'. However certain questions are unavoidable and the European Union is faced with questions that are not going to go away. Does it go for *widening* through enlargement of up to 26 members in the near future? Or does it concentrate on *deepening* so that the existing members are more and more closely integrated? Or does it move ahead on the basis that widening and deepening must go hand in hand?

The British have traditionally been keen on enlargement as a way of diluting the Community, now the Union. On the eve of Britain taking over the Presidency of the Union in January 1998 the Foreign Secretary, Robin Cook made it clear that the UK would push for rapid enlargement. Cynics argued that in the absence of British involvement in EMU, enlargement was the only theme their Presidency could offer.

In theory Parliament could repeal the 1972 European Communities Accession Act and take the UK out of the European Union although this would be to risk economic isolation, break treaty commitments and to reduce Britain's standing in the world. Relatively few politicians appear to believe that the United Kingdom should actually leave the European Union although some argue that Britain should 'repatriate' powers lost to Europe and reduce the power of the ECJ. Even fewer openly advocate moving towards a federal Europe. The majority are in favour of continued membership but with varying degrees of enthusiasm about further integration.

STUDY GUIDES

Revision Hints

This is the most contemporary of the material dealt with in the book, so it would be very useful to update your notes as events emerge. Follow the media to see what happens about enlargement and EMU, and about the British relationship with Europe in general. Of course you need to be aware that there is no such thing as a totally neutral, objective stance. If you follow events through a newspaper like *The Guardian* or *The Observer*, you are more likely to read a sympathetic account than if you turn to *The Sun* or *The Mail*. The broadcast media have an obligation to present balanced coverage, but again balance is in the eye of the beholder. Generally speaking you will find that for example Channel Four news at 7pm and Newsnight on BBC2 at 10.30pm give more detailed accounts of what is going on in Europe, than does ITV's News at Ten.

The crucial decisions on enlargement and EMU must be taken within the next year or so (from 1998), and they will generate enormous media interest. As always there is no right or wrong approach, and you need to be aware of this as you make your notes and follow events.

When answering questions on the future of EU, it is not necessary to gaze into a crystal ball; what you are required to do is to look at the implications of various courses of action. You will not be marked on the quality of your prophecy, rather, on the quality of your argument.

Consider the following titles:

1 'The United Kingdom cannot play a leading role in Europe for as long as it refuses to join Economic and Monetary Union'. Discuss.

2 'A European Union of 26 or more members cannot function effectively; the UK would be better pulling out and going it alone'. Consider the truth of this statement.

The two questions approach the issues of the future of the European Union and of Britain's role within it from very different angles. The implication of the first is that the United Kingdom remains an 'awkward member' and the government has again opted out on the most crucial issue facing the Union. Consider the importance of EMU to the future direction of the Union, and look at reasons why, for the moment at least, the UK is hesitating about committing herself.

It also needs an examination of the ways in which the UK could offer leadership in Europe even if it was not involved in EMU. There are many Euroenthusiasts, such as Lord Dahrendorf (a German academic, now a member of the House of Lords), who believe that EMU is a mistake and that it would be better for the EU if it were to seek to develop in other directions. The most obvious way in which this could happen is through enlargement.

In the second essay, you need to look at the dilemmas posed by enlarging a body originally designed for six states so that it can accommodate 26. What implications does this have for the practical functioning of the Union and in what ways might it make the organisation unworkable? In the second part of the essay, you are asked to consider the case for British withdrawal. However unlikely this may still seem in the late 1990s, it has moved up the agenda since 1992. It used to be that leaving the Community was discussed in purely theoretical terms, eg, did the fact that Parliament could repeal the 1972 Act which took Britain into Europe, prove that Parliament was still ultimately sovereign? Now it has become something which serious politicians such as the former Chancellor, Norman Lamont, openly discuss. If EMU does fail, the demands for the UK to leave the Union will become more insistent; it is therefore necessary to contemplate seriously what trading arrangements and foreign policy decisions would arise if the UK left the EU.

1 Can the UK ever be 'at the heart of Europe'?
2 Why is there more and more talk of the UK withdrawing from the European Union?

GLOSSARY

CAP – Common Agricultural Policy. The oldest and most controversial Community policy. Brought in under pressure from the French in 1962, it aims to stabilise agricultural prices.

CFP – Common Fisheries Policy. Another controversial policy, this aims at conserving stocks of fish by allocating quotas to each member state.

COREPER – The Committee of Permanent Representatives brings together the member states' ambassadors to the EU. It organises all Council and European Council meetings.

ECHR – the European Court of Human Rights.

ECJ – the European Court of Justice, the judicial wing of the EU.

ECSC – the European Coal and Steel Community.

EFTA – the European Free Trade Association.

EMU – Economic and Monetary Union. This would mean a single central bank issuing a common currency, the Euro.

EP – the European Parliament. This shares control over the budget with the Council of Ministers. It has co-decision-making powers in many areas, and this means it can amend or reject draft law.

EPC – European Political Co-operation. The term used to describe attempts at co-ordinating foreign and defence policy, now superseded by the CFSP – Common Foreign and Security Policy.

ERM – the Exchange Rate Mechanism which aims to provide a zone of currency stability in the Community by aligning exchange rates more closely together.

QMV – Qualified Majority Voting, under which each country is allocated so many votes depending on the size of its population, and where a certain number is required to approve a measure.

SEA – the Single European Act which sought to move from a common market to a single market and in so doing galvanised the Community after a decade of lethargy. The aim was completion of the internal market by 1992.

The **TEU** – the Maastricht Treaty, more properly known as the Treaty of European Union, which turned the former European Community into the European Union.

FURTHER READING

BOOKS

There are lots of books about the history, structure and operations of the EU, but the following represent the most accessible and readable.

An Awkward Partner, Stephen George (Oxford University Press, 1994) – discusses the British approach to Europe.

Politics and Policy in the European Community, S. George (Oxford University Press, 1991) – a standard short text on the way the Community operates.

The European Community; Structure and Processes, Clive Archer and Fiona Butler (Pinter Publishers, 1992) – another concise account of the way the Community functions.

Ever Closer Union? Desmond Dinan (Macmillan, 1994) – a more detailed account of the development of the EU.

The Government and Politics of the European Union, Neill Nugent (Macmillan, 1994) – one of the standard texts on the EU.

An Introduction to the European Union, Duncan Watts (Sheffield Hallam, 1996) – a thorough and balanced account of the history, institutions and policies of the EU.

NEWSPAPERS

All the 'quality press' cover European issues but with varying approaches. *The Guardian*, *The Independent* and the *Observer* tend to be more enthusiastic than *The Times* or the *Telegraph*. For obvious reasons, *The European* specialises in matters concerning the EU.

MAGAZINES

The Economist and *The New Statesman* both cover issues in detail and form a broadly pro-integrationist approach. *The Spectator* tends to be more Eurosceptic.

INDEX